WHY WE NEED VACCINES

How Humans Beat Infectious Diseases

Rowena Rae

Illustrated by
Paige Stampatori

ORCA BOOK PUBLISHERS

Published in Canada and the United States in 2024 by Orca Book Publishers.
orcabook.com

Library and Archives Canada Cataloguing in Publication
Title: Why we need vaccines : how humans beat infectious diseases / Rowena Rae ; illustrated by Paige Stampatori.
Names: Rae, Rowena, author. | Stampatori, Paige, illustrator.
Series: Orca timeline ; 6.
Description: Series statement: Orca timeline ; 6 | Includes bibliographical references and index.
Identifiers: Canadiana (print) 20230485669 | Canadiana (ebook) 20230485677 | ISBN 9781459836945 (hardcover) |
ISBN 9781459836952 (PDF) | ISBN 9781459836969 (EPUB)
Subjects: LCSH: Vaccination—Juvenile literature. | LCSH: Vaccination—Social aspects—Juvenile literature.
Classification: LCC RA638 .R34 2024 | DDC j614.4/7—dc23

Library of Congress Control Number: 2023942425

Summary: Part of the nonfiction Orca Timeline series, with photographs and illustrations throughout,
this book examines the history, science, ethics and social issues related to infectious diseases and vaccines.

Orca Book Publishers is committed to reducing the consumption of nonrenewable resources in the
production of our books. We make every effort to use materials that support a sustainable future.

Orca Book Publishers gratefully acknowledges the support for its publishing programs provided by
the following agencies: the Government of Canada, the Canada Council for the Arts and the Province
of British Columbia through the BC Arts Council and the Book Publishing Tax Credit.

Cover and interior artwork by Paige Stampatori
Design by Dahlia Yuen
Edited by Kirstie Hudson

Printed and bound in South Korea.

27 26 25 24 • 1 2 3 4

For young people everywhere,
both vaccinated and unvaccinated.

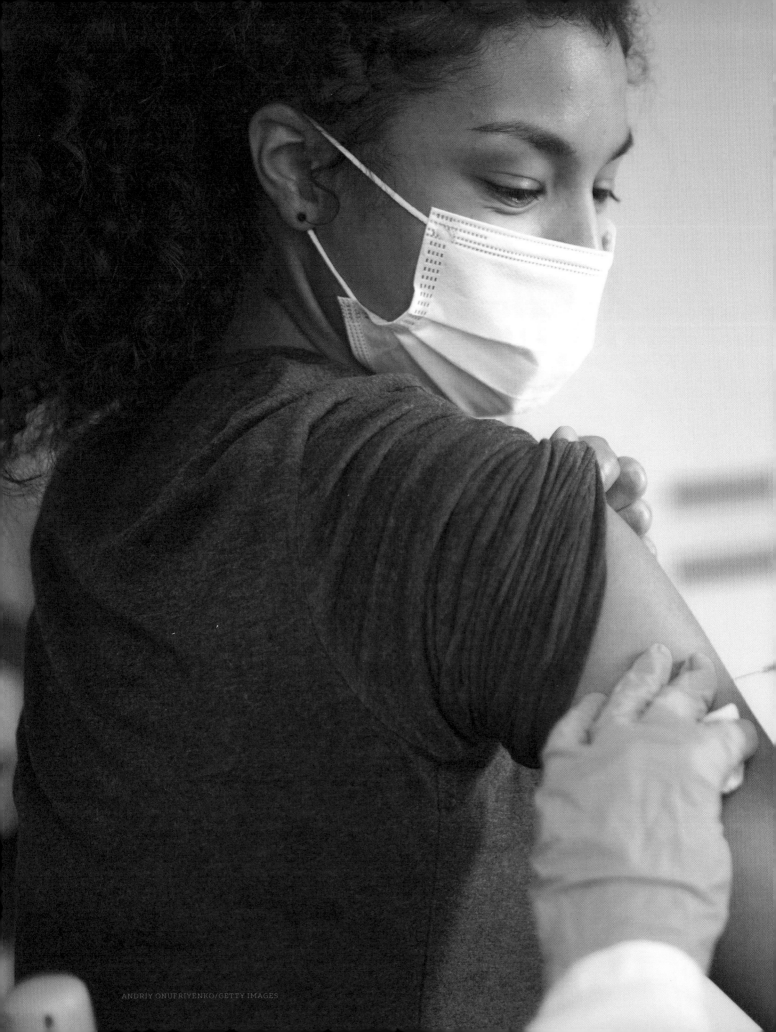

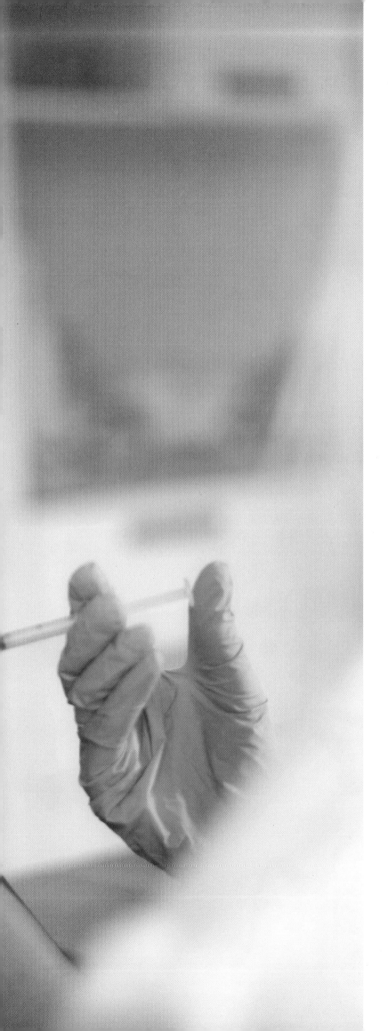

CONTENTS

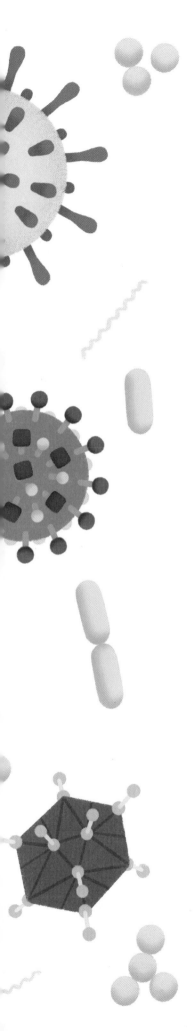

INTRODUCTION

My mother worked as a doctor of ***infectious diseases***. These are illnesses caused by tiny organisms like ***bacteria***, ***fungi***, ***protozoa*** and ***viruses***. Most of them can be seen only through a ***microscope***, so they're called micro (very small) organisms, or ***microbes*** for short. Our planet has trillions of microbes, and most of them don't harm people. But some do. The ones that enter a person's body and make them sick are the unfriendly microbes called germs, or ***pathogens***. Pathogens cause ***infections***, and many are ***contagious***—they can spread from one individual to another.

As you can tell from all the italicized bold words in just the first paragraph, this book introduces a lot of science terms. Many of these may be new to you, so please consult the glossary on pages 81–83 for definitions.

My mother spent her days looking through a microscope at pathogens from people who were feeling sick. Her job was to figure out which pathogen they had and which medicine would help them feel better. Over dinner she would tell our family about her day. We heard about awful diseases that changed people's lives. About tragedies when a medicine didn't work. And about medical mysteries, like when a new illness appeared and doctors didn't know what it was.

But we also heard about happier events. Patients who got better and went home to their families. New medicines for treating diseases. Medicines that could prevent people from getting sick in the first place. The most common of these preventive medicines are ***vaccines***.

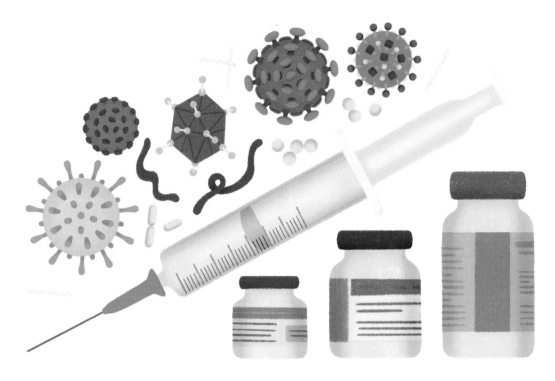

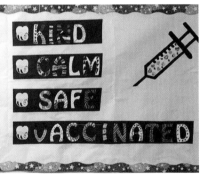

In the early days of the COVID-19 pandemic, British Columbia's health officer, Dr. Bonnie Henry, gave daily updates to the media. She ended each one by saying, "Be kind, be calm, be safe."
ROWENA RAE

Vaccines help a person's body identify and stop pathogens that are trying to make them sick. To me as a young person, the most intriguing story was about the vaccine for smallpox. For thousands of years, the smallpox virus made a lot of people very sick, leaving some with deep, pitted scars—called *pockmarks*—for life and killing others. But no more! The smallpox vaccine helped to wipe out, or *eradicate*, the virus. The smallpox virus was declared eradicated from the world when I was eight, in 1980. Today nobody in the whole world has been sick with smallpox for more than 40 years. What an amazing story! A disease that doesn't exist anymore because scientists made a vaccine and a lot of people got vaccinated with it.

As you can tell, I grew up believing in vaccines.

And then one day, as an adult, I was chatting with a friend, and she mentioned that her child wasn't vaccinated—against anything. I was stunned. I tried to explain what I knew about vaccines. I talked about all the diseases we no longer have to worry about because of successful vaccines.

I tried to explain how this is true in **developed countries** like Canada, where I live, but not in **developing countries** such as Burundi, Haiti and Yemen. Every year, about *1.5 million* people die—mostly in developing countries—from infectious diseases that could have been prevented by vaccines. Nothing I said made a difference to my friend's view of vaccines. It was a hard conversation, and I came away wanting to understand more about why some people don't get vaccinated. I realized I also had other questions. How are vaccines developed and tested? Do all vaccines work the same way? What are the risks of getting vaccinated—and of *not* getting vaccinated? How can we get vaccines to more people in the world? What is the future of vaccines?

I decided to learn as much as I could from reading and talking with experts, and then I wrote it down in this book. If you're wondering about the answers to those questions, then read on!

Oh, and after all my reading, talking and learning, I still believe in vaccines. Even more now than before.

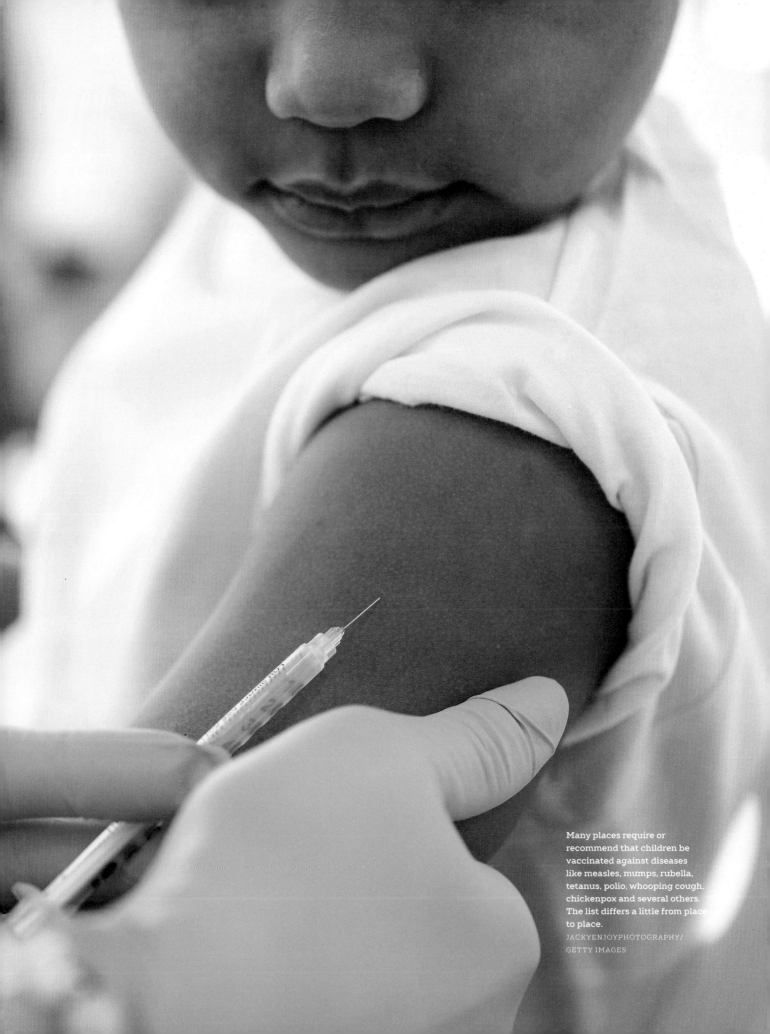

Many places require or recommend that children be vaccinated against diseases like measles, mumps, rubella, tetanus, polio, whooping cough, chickenpox and several others. The list differs a little from place to place.
JACKYENJOYPHOTOGRAPHY/ GETTY IMAGES

1157 BCE
Early recorded diseases

1347
Black Death

1918
WW1 soldiers bring
Spanish flu home

1940s
Polio

ONE

ANXIETY

When Pathogens Thrive and Spread

When my youngest daughter was five, she got an infection that sent her to hospital for a week. She had infectious bacteria growing out of control inside her body. The doctors tried a few different antibiotics—medicines that fight bacteria—until finally one worked, and she got better.

It was a terrible, scary week.

But we were lucky—lucky to live now, when treatments exist for many infectious diseases. For most of the time that humans have lived on Earth, there were no such treatments. If you got sick with an infectious disease, your body's *immune system* had to fight the disease as best as it could. Some people lived, some died. That was life, and death.

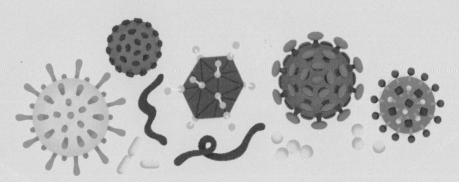

Epidemics of the Past

Bacteria, viruses and other pathogens have always infected people, right from when early humans walked on Earth. We don't know much about the pathogens that infected people thousands of years ago. But 3,000-year-old Egyptian mummies have been found with pockmarks on their skin. And ancient writings from China and India describe a disease similar to smallpox. Infectious diseases flourished when people began farming. By growing crops and raising animals, people could live in one place instead of roaming the land hunting and gathering foods. As more people settled together in towns, the crowding allowed pathogens to spread easily and quickly.

When an infectious disease spreads widely, it's called an *epidemic*. One of the first recorded epidemics tore through the Roman Empire in the years 165 to 262. It was probably the smallpox virus. Centuries later an infectious bacterium swept through Europe. In five years it killed at least 25 million people—maybe more. This epidemic, called the Black Death, started in 1347 and ended several years later. The same bacterium kept returning for many more centuries. Each time, it claimed more lives. These and other diseases traveled with people— and, in the case of the Black Death, with rats and fleas—as they moved across and between Africa, Asia and Europe.

During the Black Death, also called bubonic plague, doctors wore outfits with masks shaped like a bird's beak to allow them to keep sweet-smelling herbs or spices near their noses and mouths. In those days, people thought diseases were caused by bad-smelling air. There were also wagons called "dead carts" used to pick up the bodies of people who had died from the plague.
WIKIMEDIA COMMONS/PUBLIC DOMAIN

THANAMAT SOMWAN/SHUTTERSTOCK.COM

Handwashing Turns 150

Only a few years ago, in 2017, handwashing had its 150th birthday. Although it's almost impossible to believe now, up until the mid-1800s, doctors and surgeons never washed their hands or medical instruments. Not surprisingly, most hospital patients with open wounds ended up with infections. Some hospitals even considered banning surgeries because so many patients died!

Joseph Lister, an English doctor, was the first to realize that washing hands and instruments meant fewer wound infections and better healing. He used a weak acid for washing and required others working with him to do the same. In 1867 he wrote two medical articles about his technique and results. Today we know that handwashing is important not only in hospitals but for all of us in daily life—after using the washroom, before eating or preparing food and after being in public places like buses and stores.

1492–1800s

A Consequence of Colonization

People from Europe began arriving in and colonizing the place they called the "New World"—the Caribbean islands and the American continents—in the late 1490s, bringing with them animals, plants, insects and—disastrously—pathogens. The pathogens included the microbes that cause smallpox, measles, mumps, influenza and other diseases. In the 1600s enslaved people were forcibly transported from Africa to the Americas, and with them came other pathogens, including the ones that cause malaria and yellow fever.

The Indigenous Peoples in the Americas were not *immune* to these new diseases—their bodies didn't have any past experience at fighting off the infections. The result was devastating. These imported diseases spread to the Indigenous Peoples, making many of them sick. Some people survived their illnesses, but since the start of colonization, millions of Indigenous people in the Americas lost their lives to these infectious diseases.

> In 1800 life expectancy—the average number of years a person could expect to live—was about 30 years. Most people died of infectious diseases.

Modern Epidemics

A particularly deadly outbreak of influenza happened in 1918, causing a *pandemic*—a disease that affects the whole world. That year also marked the end of World War I. Soldiers and others returning home from the battlefields in Europe brought the influenza virus with them. Often called the Spanish flu (even though it didn't start in Spain), this influenza pandemic killed about 50 million people worldwide.

A few decades later, during the late 1940s and into the 1950s, the poliovirus returned every few years. One form of this terrible disease can paralyze a person's legs for life. In the worst cases, the muscles that control the lungs become paralyzed. People who developed this frightening complication had to live in *ventilator* machines called iron lungs, which mechanically inflated and deflated their chests.

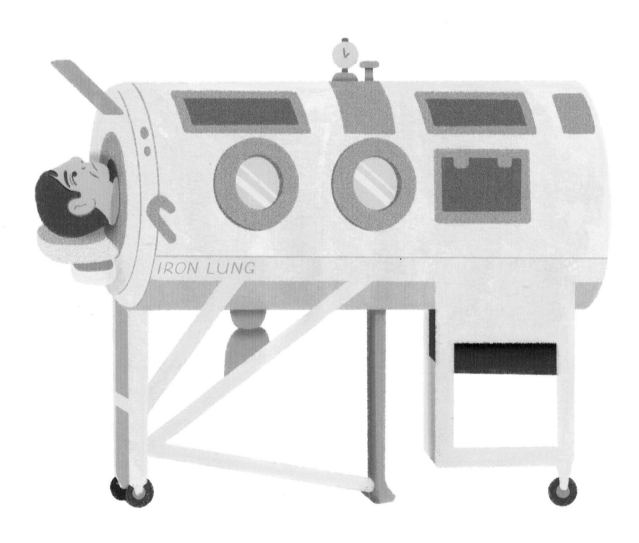

IRON LUNG

Main Causes of Death

*per 100,000 people

1900 (start of the 20th century)

#1 Pneumonia and influenza
202.2*

#2 Tuberculosis
194.4*

#3 Diarrheal disease
142.7*

1998 (end of the 20th century)

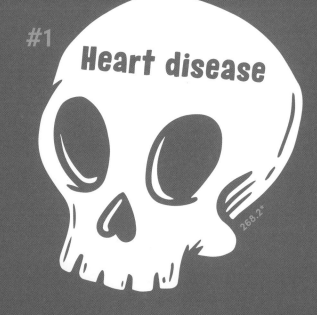

#1 Heart disease
268.2*

#2 Cancers
200.3*

#3 Stroke
58.6*

The data above is from the United States. In 1900, infectious microbes were behind all three of the top causes of death. A century later, in 1998, the top causes had changed. Why the difference? The reasons include better access to clean water, improved hygiene and living conditions, better nutrition, more-advanced medical care and the discovery of antibiotics, other kinds of medicine and vaccines. The data differs from country to country, but most developed nations have a similar story.

DATA FROM THE CENTERS FOR DISEASE CONTROL AND PREVENTION (CDC), ACCESSED FROM OURWORLDINDATA.ORG/CAUSES-OF-DEATH.

Coronaviruses

Many infectious diseases are caused by pathogens that have jumped from animals to humans. These diseases are called *zoonoses*—*zoo* means "animal," and *nosos* means "disease." In late 2019 a coronavirus seems to have jumped from an animal—possibly a bat—in China and infected a person. The virus, named SARS-CoV-2 (severe acute respiratory syndrome from coronavirus number 2), causes the disease called COVID-19. It took the world by storm after spreading in China and then moving to other countries when infected people traveled by airplane.

Within just a few months, the World Health Organization declared a pandemic. Country after country shut its borders and told its citizens to stay at home.

Doctors and other healthcare workers scrambled to treat the desperately sick patients who struggled to breathe. Hospitals filled up, equipment was in short supply, and hundreds of thousands of people died. Scientists rushed to learn as much as they could about this new virus so they could find treatments—and, better yet, a vaccine.

But that's getting ahead of the story.

At the beginning of the COVID-19 pandemic, officials shut down public spaces and told people to stay at home. Even outdoor playgrounds were closed! RAINSTAR/GETTY IMAGES

Alexandre White

EM JOSEPH

"Read as much as you can. Ask questions. And follow what you're interested in. If one interest fades, then follow another one and see where it takes you."

As a kid **Alexandre White** wanted to become a heart surgeon or go into politics. Then he went to college and discovered how much he enjoyed his classes in Black studies and history. He became interested in how and why different groups of people have unequal access to healthcare. For example, some people don't receive the same quality of healthcare as others. This is often the case for members of racialized or marginalized groups. They are at greater risk of being dismissed, ignored and left undiagnosed for diseases, which can lead to higher rates of illness and lower life expectancy. "Our health exists within the social inequalities we live in," White says.

White now works as a university professor in history and sociology. His speciality is studying infectious-disease outbreaks, both past and present, to find out how different people have been treated. He does his work by interviewing health experts and visiting archives—places that house diaries, letters and other historical documents—in Switzerland, England and several African countries. "I travel a lot and often have my nose in some dusty set of reports from way back when!" White says.

With the information he collects, White writes books and essays. "I work to uncover and confront histories of inequality in healthcare. I look at questions of racism, colonialism and healthcare access," he says. "I want to help prevent these things from happening in the future."

Future
Not All Doom and Gloom

This chapter has been full of sickness and death. Sadly, these are the realities of infectious diseases in humans. And if history is anything to go by, infectious diseases will continue to make people sick and anxious well into the future. These are not easy things to read about.

Also keep in mind that it's not all doom and gloom! Scientists are busy studying pathogens and looking for new treatments and vaccines. And you can do lots of things to lessen your anxiety about infectious diseases, keep yourself and your family as safe as possible and help your community. As well as getting vaccinated, you can help protect yourself and others by washing your hands, covering your nose and mouth when you cough or sneeze, wearing a mask in public and staying home when you're feeling sick.

What worries you about infectious diseases? What makes you hopeful?

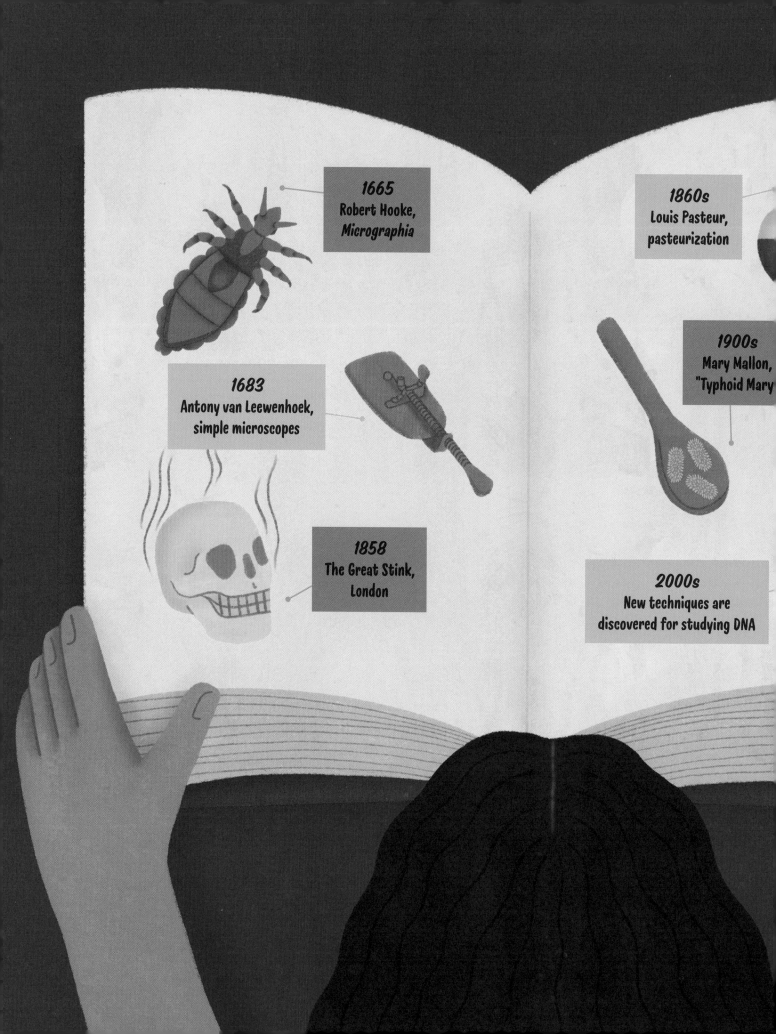

TWO

CURIOSITY

When People Look for Answers

In the summer of 1858 the horrible stench of human sewage wafted up from the River Thames and hung over London. The Great Stink, as it was known, filled people with fear. At the time, many people thought that revolting smells caused disease. They were especially afraid of cholera, which causes severe diarrhea, dehydration and often death. Waves of cholera kept surfacing in the 1800s. But although revolting smells are, well, revolting, they aren't the reason people get sick. The reason, as we now know, is infectious microbes, or pathogens. But nobody knew then that microbes even existed, in part because they couldn't see them. For this "small" piece of the story, we travel to Holland for a "micro" discovery.

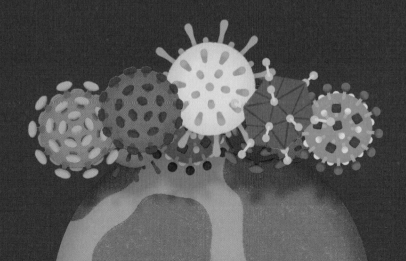

Seeing the Tiny

If you had trouble seeing 400 or so years ago, an eyeglass maker could make you a pair of glasses with polished lenses to enlarge the view of, or magnify, objects. Some Dutch eyeglass makers in about 1590 experimented with placing a lens at each end of a tube. When they looked through the tube, the two lenses worked together to magnify an object even more. This instrument was the first microscope.

Nobody paid much attention to this new "toy" until Robert Hooke, an English natural scientist, used a microscope to examine nature. He published a book, *Micrographia*, in 1665 with detailed drawings of insects, plant *cells* and much more. Hooke even let a louse bite

his finger while he watched through a microscope as his own blood flowed into the louse's body!

The next person to make a huge— well, actually a really tiny—discovery using a microscope was Antony van Leewenhoek, a Dutch man who may have been inspired by *Micrographia*. He learned how to polish lenses so that he could see small things for himself: a drop of pond water, the muscle of a codfish, even the plaque from his teeth. After observing one of his samples, he wrote in 1683 that he saw "many very little living animalcules, very prettily a-moving." These "animalcules," or little animals, were bacteria.

BACTERIA
- Free-living cells
- Live inside or outside a body
- Multiply on their own, usually by *binary fission*
- Small, but much larger than viruses
- Have DNA as their genetic material

BOTH
All around us

Too small to see with the naked eye

Come in many different shapes

Some cause disease

Cause similar symptoms of infection

Some benefit people or animals

Some can be prevented with vaccines

VIRUS
- Non-living collections of molecules
- Need a host to survive
- Multiply only by entering a living cell and forcing it to make copies of the virus
- Very small, much smaller than bacteria
- Have DNA or RNA as their genetic material

BACTERIA and VIRUSES have big differences and also many similarities.

Making Connections

In the 1860s Louis Pasteur, a French chemist, puzzled over soured wine and beer. By experimenting, he realized that liquids (and other things) don't just go bad on their own. They go bad because microbes from the air, such as bacteria and fungi, **contaminate** them. Pasteur invented a way of heating wine or beer for a short time and then cooling it back down. This process—called **pasteurization**—killed the microbes that soured the drinks.

Not long afterward, Robert Koch, a German scientist, was investigating anthrax, a disease that often killed farm animals. He found microbes shaped like short rods in the blood of sick cows. He injected this tainted blood into one group of mice, and blood from healthy cows into another group of mice. The mice that got the infected blood became sick with anthrax, while the other mice did not.

What Pasteur and Koch learned from their work is called the germ theory of disease—the understanding that one type of germ (pathogen) causes one disease. Knowing this, scientists started looking for treatments and preventions targeted at specific pathogens.

Some pathogens are more contagious than others.

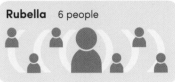

Measles is especially contagious—one sick person typically infects at least 12 other people, on average. Rubella and mumps are less contagious, but one sick person can still infect several other people. DATA FROM S.A. PLOTKIN, W.A. ORENSTEIN, P.A. OFFIT, *VACCINES*, 5TH ED., ELSEVIER INC. 2008.

Louis Pasteur at work in his laboratory. Pasteur contributed so much to science that if he had lived in a time when Nobel Prizes were awarded, he probably would have received one—or more. But he died six years before the first Nobel Prize was awarded, in 1901. MIKROMAN6/GETTY IMAGES

One way to identify bacteria is to grow them on agar, a jelly-like substance made from red algae. A layer of agar in a petri dish—a flat, round dish with a lid—provides nutrition for bacteria to grow. The dish's shape makes it easy to view the bacteria through a microscope.
TED HOROWITZ PHOTOGRAPHY/GETTY IMAGES

The Curious Case of Mary Mallon

Mary Mallon worked as a household servant and cook for wealthy families in New York State in the early 1900s. Wherever she worked, family members and servants became sick with typhoid fever. Some of them died. But Mallon never got sick. She was a carrier—in her body she had the bacteria that cause typhoid fever, but they didn't make her sick. When she cooked, bacteria from her hands got into the food and infected the people eating it. Eventually the authorities tracked her down, arrested her and forced her to live in *quarantine*. Mallon became known to the public as "Typhoid Mary."

2000s–Today
Studying Microbes

For decades after Pasteur's and Koch's discoveries, scientists searched for the microbes responsible for causing all sorts of infectious diseases. They learned to tell microbes apart by their size—bacteria are much bigger than viruses, for example. And they also examined their shapes—bacteria can look like balls, rods, corkscrews or even commas. For a long time scientists studied microbes one by one. They grew large numbers of a particular microbe in flasks and on dishes to study them. They grouped and named microbes by their physical traits—their shape and color and how they multiplied, such as in clusters or in branches.

In the early 2000s scientists developed new techniques to study *DNA*—the *inherited* instructions inside cells for how an organism looks and functions. Using the new techniques, scientists can go beyond physical traits to learn how microbes behave, what they make and how they interact with one another.

Scientists can now study whole *communities* of microbes. The difference between studying microbes of one type, or *species*, at a time versus studying whole communities is similar to the difference between watching one bird species at a seed feeder versus watching several bird species all feeding—or squabbling over the seeds—at the same time. You often learn more by watching the group of different species interacting.

Did you know that, inside your body, you have about 10 bacteria for every one of your cells? And that's not all. Viruses, fungi and other microbes also call your body home. Many of these microbes don't harm us. In fact, several of them *help* us! Some make vitamins or help release nutrients from food. Some even produce substances to help us fight off pathogens.

Future

On the Lookout

As you read in chapter 1, many infectious diseases are zoonoses—diseases caused by pathogens that spread from animals to humans. With the new DNA techniques, scientists can examine microbe communities in animals and other environments to find and track pathogens that may jump to people and cause disease. This advance warning will enable other scientists to start developing treatments and vaccines before these pathogens become a threat to human health. Human health is closely connected with animal health and environmental health. As the world's population grows, people are moving into new areas, and more and more wild habitats are being taken over for human uses. These changes mean that more people are living near wild animals, and many other people also have close contact with domesticated farm animals and pets. Both of these situations increase the opportunities for pathogens to jump from wild or domestic animals to humans. To focus on the connections between people, animals and the environment, public health workers often use the term *One Health*. How do you think this term could bring people together to find ways to stop or slow down animal-to-human spread of infectious diseases?

ON THE JOB

Jaris Swidrovich

"I was involved in acting in high school," says Jaris Swidrovich. "And I also had a doctor-tickle in my brain." They enrolled in a university drama program but at the last minute switched into a science program. That led Swidrovich to study pharmacy and, later, become the first Indigenous person in Canada to become a doctor of pharmacy. After graduating, they worked for a while in a pharmacy store and then as a hospital pharmacist helping people living with *HIV/AIDS*.

Now Swidrovich is on a mission. "I have this responsibility to share information about Indigenous and queer communities with other people working in pharmacy," they say. They helped start an organization to support Indigenous Peoples working in pharmacy and encourage young people to enter this field. Swidrovich wants young people to know that working in pharmacy isn't so much about doing chemistry as it is about working with and helping people. "You have an enormous opportunity to help people with their medications, their vaccines," they say. "In pharmacy, you can be in healthcare without the blood and guts."

"Find something that inspires you. At the end of the day, success isn't your title. You need health and happiness."

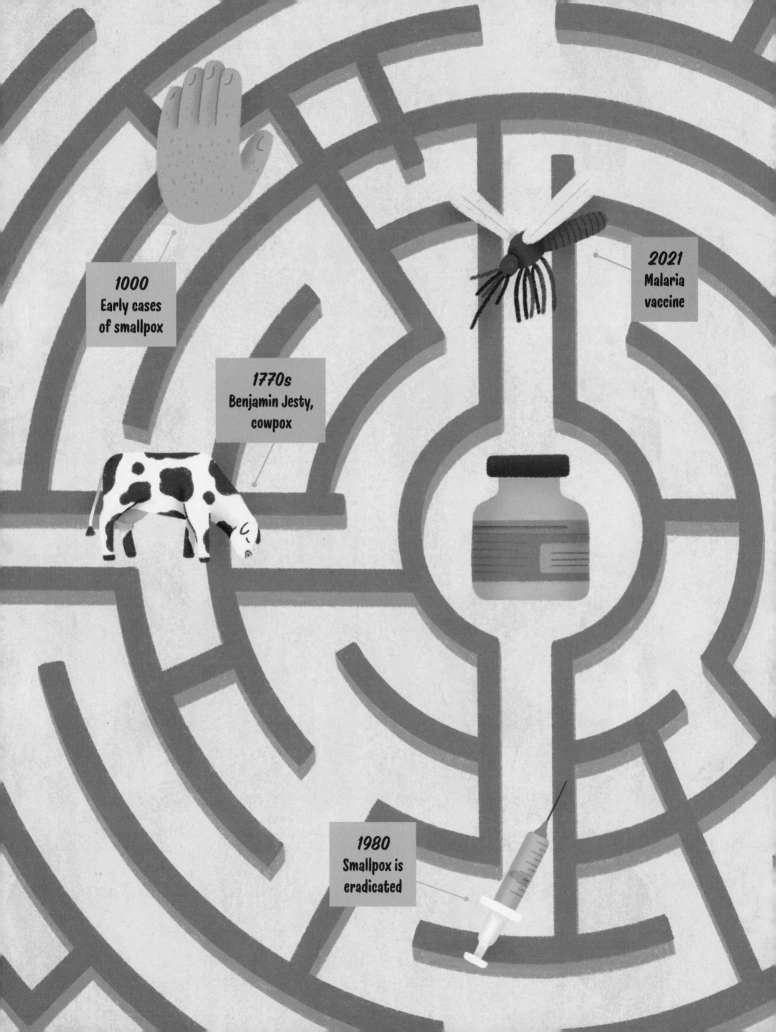

THREE

DETERMINATION

When People Look for Solutions

In this book's introduction, you read that smallpox no longer exists because so many people received the vaccine. Unlike most of today's vaccines, the smallpox vaccine left a scar—mine is about the size of a Smartie on my left upper arm. I was one of the last Canadian children vaccinated, because routine smallpox *vaccination* ended in Canada, the United States and some other countries in the early 1970s. Smallpox was the first infectious disease to be eradicated, and it was also the first with a vaccine. Let's find out how the vaccine came to be.

1000–1700s

Transferring Disease

Long before anyone knew about microbes, they had a basic understanding of **immunity**. Immunity refers to how the body protects itself from infectious diseases. Even thousands of years ago, it was known that some people got very sick with a disease and died, but others got sick and survived. Of every ten people who got smallpox, about three died. The survivors often had terrible scars, but they didn't get sick with smallpox for a second time.

This basic understanding was enough for some people to experiment with a technique called **variolation** (pronounced VARE-ee-oh-lay-shun). This word comes from another name for the smallpox virus, variola virus.

Variolation involved scraping—warning: this is pretty gross!—pus or scabs from blisters on a sick person's skin and wiping them into small scratches on a healthy person's skin or even poking them into their nose. Eew! The person being variolated would usually get a mild case of smallpox, and once they recovered, they had immunity against the disease.

About a thousand years ago, people were already using variolation to protect against smallpox in many parts of the world, such as India, China and the Ottoman Empire (parts of today's Eastern Europe, Middle East and Africa). In the 1700s the technique spread to Britain and the United States.

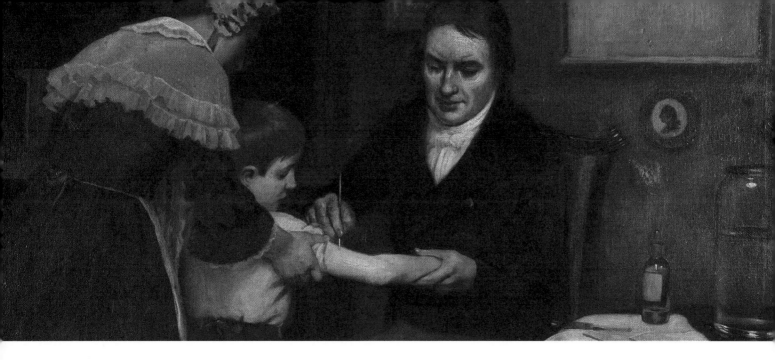

1770s–1800
A Dairy Discovery

Have you ever seen a cow milked by hand? The person milking the cow sits very close to the animal and pulls on her teats to squirt milk from the udder into a bucket. A disease in cows, called cowpox, causes blisters on the udders, so dairy workers milking many cows a day were often exposed to this disease and got blisters on their hands and arms. The cowpox virus, also called vaccinia virus, happens to be related to the smallpox virus. Why does that matter? It turns out that dairy workers rarely got sick from smallpox, even when they were exposed to it. By getting cowpox, dairy workers seemed to have immunity against smallpox.

Benjamin Jesty, an English farmer, realized this in the 1770s—and other farmers probably did too. Jesty purposely gave his wife and two sons cowpox using the variolation technique. They all stayed healthy during later smallpox epidemics.

A few decades later, Edward Jenner, an English doctor, performed this same test on an eight-year-old boy—but Jenner went one step further. First he variolated the boy with cowpox (or horsepox, another related virus, according to some sources). About two months later he purposely tried to infect the boy with smallpox. The boy didn't get sick. Jenner tested more people, and none of them got smallpox when he tried to give it to them or when a natural smallpox outbreak occurred. Jesty and Jenner had done the world's first vaccinations. This word comes from *vaccine*, which can be traced to the Latin word *vacca*, meaning "cow."

Edward Jenner performed his first vaccination on eight-year-old James Phipps on May 14, 1796. This painting was done by Ernest Board, who lived a century later.

Cases of both chickenpox and measles in the United States went down after the introduction of an effective vaccine.

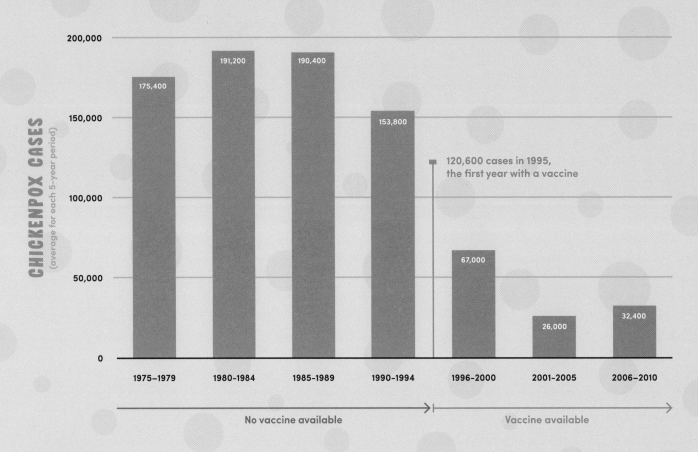

CHICKENPOX CASES (average for each 5-year period)

175,400	191,200	190,400	153,800	67,000	26,000	32,400
1975–1979	1980–1984	1985–1989	1990–1994	1996–2000	2001–2005	2006–2010

120,600 cases in 1995, the first year with a vaccine

No vaccine available → | Vaccine available →

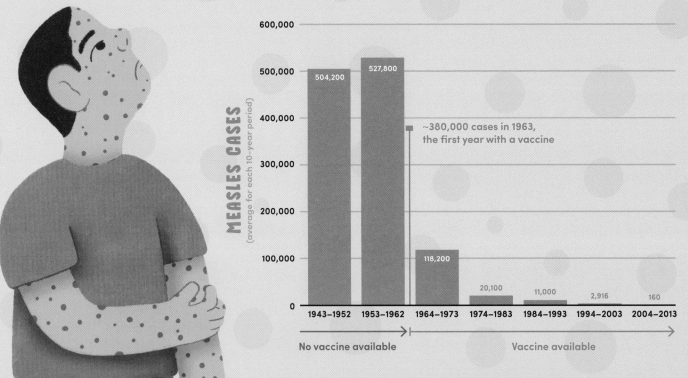

MEASLES CASES (average for each 10-year period)

504,200	527,800	118,200	20,100	11,000	2,916	160
1943–1952	1953–1962	1964–1973	1974–1983	1984–1993	1994–2003	2004–2013

~380,000 cases in 1963, the first year with a vaccine

No vaccine available → | Vaccine available →

DATA FOR CHICKENPOX FROM THE CENTERS FOR DISEASE CONTROL AND PREVENTION (CDC). DATA FOR MEASLES FROM THE US PUBLIC HEALTH SERVICE (PHS) AND THE US CENSUS. DATA ACCESSED VIA VACCINES. PROCON.ORG/VACCINE-HISTORIES-AND-IMPACT/VARICELLA-CHICKENPOX AND OURWORLDINDATA.ORG/ MICROBES-BATTLE-SCIENCE-VACCINES.

Vaccine Discoveries Take Off

The next big leap in vaccine discovery came in the 1880s with Louis Pasteur—the pasteurization man. In his science lab, Pasteur and his colleagues discovered different ways to weaken infectious bacteria. Pasteur was able to weaken bacteria enough to use them as a vaccine. Having a dramatic flair, he showed off his discovery with public experiments in France. He got five dozen farm animals—sheep, cows and goats—and divided them into two groups. One group got the newly made anthrax vaccine, and the other didn't. Two weeks later he tried to infect all the animals with anthrax bacteria. The unvaccinated animals became ill, and most of them died that same day. But the vaccinated animals didn't get anthrax disease.

> From 1900 to 1980, about 300 million people died from smallpox. That's 3.75 million (3,750,000) people dying from this single disease every year. Every year! That's the entire population of the state of Connecticut or the city of Berlin.

Not long after this experiment, Pasteur used his lab methods on a virus. He weakened the virus that causes rabies and made a vaccine against this deadly animal disease too. Over the next century, scientists developed so many new vaccines that I don't have space to tell the story of each one. Here are some of them:

1890s
- cholera
- typhoid
- diphtheria
- bubonic plague *(the bacterial disease of the Black Death)*

1910s
- pertussis *(also called whooping cough)*

1920s
- tuberculosis

1930s
- yellow fever
- tetanus

1940s
- influenza *(flu)*

1950s
- polio

1960s
- measles
- mumps
- rubella

1970s
- pneumococcus

1980s
- hepatitis B

1990s
- hepatitis A
- chickenpox
- Lyme disease

2000s
- shingles
- human papilloma virus

2020s
- COVID-19
- malaria

Wiping Out Smallpox

In 1977 Ali Maow Maalin was a 23-year-old hospital cook in Somalia. Being scared of needles, he wasn't vaccinated against smallpox. One day he rode in a car with two children infected with the disease. Bad idea—although he may not have realized the children were ill. Within a few days, he was sick with smallpox. Maalin survived the disease, and he gained a dubious honor—he was the last person in the world to get sick from wild-type smallpox. *Wild-type* means the virus was out in the community so Maalin contracted it from another person. (This differs from how an English woman became infected the following year when smallpox virus leaked out of a medical lab in England.)

A decade before Maalin got smallpox, the World Health Organization (WHO) had launched an ambitious campaign to rid the world of the disease. After an enormous amount of work, money, disease tracking and vaccinations, the campaign succeeded. In May 1980 the WHO declared the world free of smallpox—the first disease eradicated. So far it's still the only human one. (Rinderpest virus, which infected and killed cattle, buffalo and other cloven-hoofed animals, was declared eradicated in 2011.)

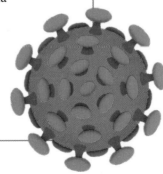

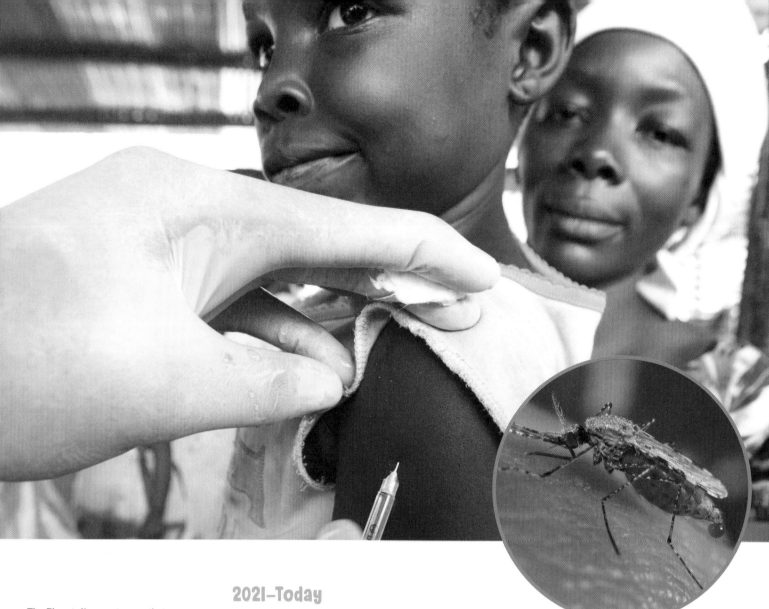

The *Plasmodium* protozoan that causes malaria is a parasite carried by female *Anopheles* mosquitoes. When the mosquito takes a meal of blood from a human, the mosquito can pass the parasite to the person. The parasite doesn't harm the mosquito.
CREDIT: (MAIN) HEREWARD HOLLAND/REUTERS; (INSET) JIM GATHANY/CDC/PUBLIC DOMAIN

2021–Today
Problematic Protozoan

Something exciting happened in December 2021—the world's first malaria vaccine got approved. Malaria makes more than 200 million people sick *every year*, and about 400,000 of those people die—many of them children younger than five. The cause of malaria is a protozoan—a small animal that has just one cell—called *Plasmodium*. Mosquitoes carry *Plasmodium* and give it to people, mostly in Africa but elsewhere too.

Making a malaria vaccine has been tricky, in part because *Plasmodium* has many stages in its life cycle. In fact, malaria is the first protozoan-caused disease with a vaccine against it. This first malaria vaccine protects 30 to 40 percent of vaccinated people. But wait—most vaccines against viral and bacterial diseases protect 80 to 90 percent of vaccinated people. So why is the malaria vaccine so exciting? Malaria affects so many people that stopping just 30 percent of infections means saving 120,000 lives each year.

In April 2023 an improved malaria vaccine became available. It protects about 75 percent of vaccinated people. By the time you read this book, there may be an even *better* malaria vaccine.

Taking Vaccines Further

In the space of 250 years, people's curiosity has taken the world from the first smallpox vaccinations in the English countryside to the development of dozens of effective and safe vaccines. What else is coming? A lot, and it won't take 250 years.

Several infectious diseases still don't have effective vaccines, especially many tropical diseases, such as Zika and chikungunya. And more diseases will emerge that we don't know about yet. As well as tackling vaccines against infectious diseases, scientists have ideas about using vaccines in other ways. They're working to develop vaccines that will prevent many different *cancers* and treat *autoimmune disorders*.

What do you think the world could look like in about 250 years—in the 2270s—with vaccines of the future?

ON THE JOB

Akarin Asavajaru

DAVID STOBBE, VIDO/USASK

When he was younger, Akarin Asavajaru wanted to be a singer or an actor in movies. But then, in high school, his science teacher sparked his passion for asking questions and doing science experiments. "Science gives me answers," says Asavajaru. "I find out things I want to know."

Now, as a research technician at the University of Saskatchewan's Vaccine and Infectious Disease Organization, he's asking really big questions: Why do some viruses make people very sick but they don't affect the bats that carry them? What is it about a bat's immune system that protects it? To answer these questions, Asavajaru and other researchers work together doing experiments in a lab.

And when they've answered those questions, what might be next? "I want to try to find a way to protect us from these viruses," says Asavajaru. "I want to help develop vaccines. Vaccines are the way to protect people."

"Some kids think science is boring. But it's not; it's cool. You can be a cool kid in science."

1880s
Immune system
is discovered

1955
Jonas Salk,
polio vaccine

2000s
mRNA is used
in vaccines

1890s
First killed/
inactivated vaccine

1960s
Oral vaccines
for children

CLEVERNESS

How Vaccines Work

I remember sitting in a doctor's office at about age five. The doctor handed me a sugar cube and told me I could eat it. What a treat! I popped the cube in my mouth and sucked as it quickly dissolved. I didn't know it then, but I had just swallowed a polio vaccine. Polio is the disease I mentioned in chapter 1—the one that paralyzes some of its victims.

Fifteen years after my polio vaccination, I was a biology student at university. One of my classmates wore clunky metal braces on both legs and used crutches. As she walked, her upper body swayed and jerked, left, right, left, right. This classmate was born in Sri Lanka, a developing country, and she'd had polio as a child. From her I got a glimpse of polio's severe consequences. I also realized that by the good luck of where I was born, I got a vaccine to protect me. Because of my classmate's birthplace, she didn't, and she suffered this preventable disease.

Because of polio vaccination, we don't often see people walking in leg braces or hear of someone living long-term with a ventilator (today's iron lung). Polio is invisible to us because vaccines have been so effective.

So how do vaccines work?

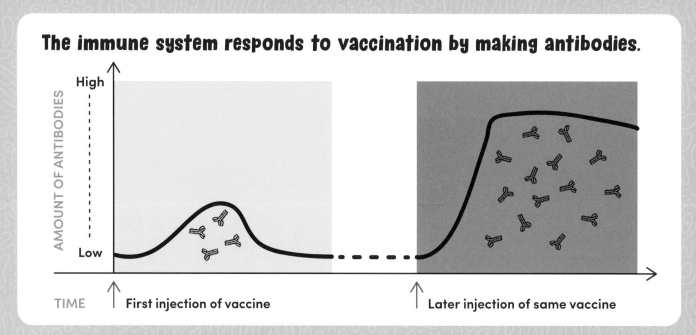

The immune system responds to vaccination by making antibodies.

AMOUNT OF ANTIBODIES
High
Low

TIME
↑ First injection of vaccine

↑ Later injection of same vaccine

The first time someone gets a particular vaccine, their body responds by making antibodies. Often the amount, or concentration, of antibodies goes down over time, so the person needs another dose of the vaccine. When they get the next dose, their body recognizes the vaccine and responds faster and more strongly. This next dose of vaccine is sometimes called a "booster" because it boosts the person's immunity.

ADAPTED FROM "THE SCIENCE OF IMMUNISATION: QUESTIONS AND ANSWERS," *AUSTRALIAN ACADEMY OF SCIENCE*, CANBERRA, 2021. SCIENCE.ORG.AU/IMMUNISATION

1880s–1920s
Discovering the Immune System

To understand how vaccines work, it helps to know a little about the immune system—the body's approach to keeping us healthy by looking for anything out of the ordinary, such as pathogens that could make us sick. Several parts of the body help with this. First there's our largest organ, the skin. Its job is to physically prevent pathogens from getting into the body. The linings of our nose, throat and intestines do this job too. But sometimes a pathogen *does* get into the body and starts to multiply, causing an infection. In the 1880s a Russian scientist named Ilya Mechnikov discovered that when an organism gets infected with a pathogen, white blood cells in the bloodstream act like first responders at an accident. They do their best to clean up and get rid of pathogens by ingesting them (taking the pathogen inside themselves) and then digesting them (breaking the pathogen down).

If the pathogen resists or avoids these "first-responder cells," then another type of white blood cell makes ***antibodies***. The antibodies attach to the pathogen and shut it down. Antibodies are like keys—only one shape works for each type of pathogen. Antibodies for the whooping cough pathogen have a different shape than the antibodies for the tuberculosis pathogen, and so on. After the immune system makes antibodies against a pathogen for the first time, it uses memory cells to recognize that pathogen if it enters the body again. This way the immune system can make antibodies more quickly the next time. Vaccines give the immune system a head start in recognizing a particular pathogen and knowing which antibodies to make to shut it down.

In 1901 the first-ever Nobel Prize in Physiology or Medicine was awarded to Emil von Behring from Prussia, who was one of the first scientists to start figuring out how the immune system works. Since then at least a dozen Nobel Prizes have honored scientists studying the immune system and immunity.

1880s+

Weakening Pathogens

The vaccines Louis Pasteur and his colleagues made against anthrax and rabies in the 1880s were *live, weakened vaccines*. These vaccines were made with a weakened form of a pathogen. Common examples of live, weakened vaccines are those for measles, mumps, rubella and chickenpox. When this type of vaccine is injected into a person, the pathogen is too weak to cause disease. But the immune system still detects the weak pathogen as unfriendly, produces antibodies and creates memory cells. The memory cells remember the pathogen for decades or even a lifetime, so if it enters the body again, they recognize it and act quickly to shut it down.

One scientist—an American vaccinologist named Maurice Hilleman—developed more than 40 vaccines, including those for measles, mumps, rubella and chickenpox.

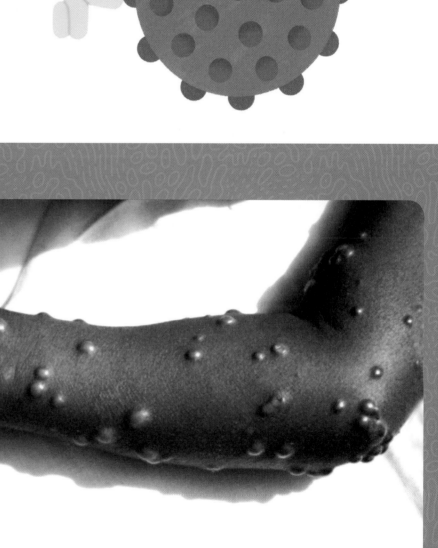

A child's arm and hand covered with smallpox lesions.
GADO IMAGES/ALAMY STOCK PHOTO

Children line up with their parents to get their polio vaccine on May 8, 1956.
FOX PHOTOS/GETTY IMAGES

POLIO VACCINATION ONLY

ENQUIRIES, FOODS, EAR, NOSE & THROAT CLINIC, USE OTHER DOOR PLEASE.

1890s–1950s+
Killing Pathogens

Within a decade of making the live, weakened vaccines against anthrax and rabies, scientists asked a different question. Would the immune system also recognize a vaccine made with a dead pathogen? The answer was yes! A pathogen can be killed with heat or chemicals and then used as a vaccine. When this vaccine is injected into the body, the immune system recognizes the dead pathogen as unfriendly and makes antibodies against it. The memory prompted by these **killed vaccines** isn't as strong as the memory from live, weakened vaccines. This is why we need multiple doses of some vaccines.

The first killed vaccines were made in the 1890s against the bacteria that cause typhoid, cholera and plague. But perhaps the most famous story is from the 1950s, when scientists in the United States raced to make a vaccine against polio.

The stakes were high. Poliovirus kept breaking out, especially in the summer, and it was children who most often caught the virus. Some of them became paralyzed for life. Some had to live in iron lungs. Some died. People avoided crowded places like festivals and swimming pools for fear of their kids getting polio. The peak was in 1952, with 57,879 Americans getting polio and 3,145 dying.

In April 1955, as another summer of sickness loomed, Jonas Salk and his team of scientists announced that they had successfully made a killed-polio vaccine. People cheered when they heard the news. A vaccination program started almost immediately across the United States and in other countries. A few years later Albert Sabin and his team of scientists successfully made a live, weakened polio vaccine that children could take by mouth (no needle in the arm!).

By 1962 the United States had fewer than 1,000 polio cases and 60 deaths. The numbers kept going down until, in 2000, both numbers were zero.

ON THE JOB

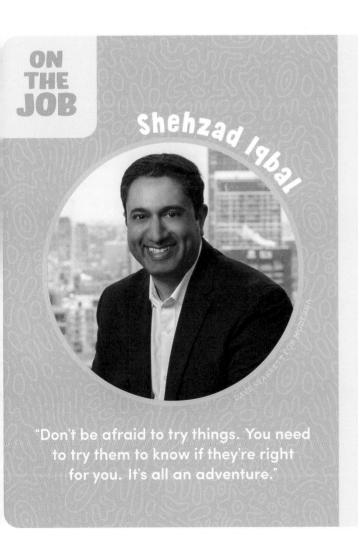

Shehzad Iqbal

DAVE SCARRETT FOR MODERNA

"Don't be afraid to try things. You need to try them to know if they're right for you. It's all an adventure."

When he was a kid, Shehzad Iqbal visited the genetics lab where one of his mom's friends worked. She showed him how to use a microscope to see tiny things that weren't visible with just his eyes. One of the tiny things he saw that day was a chromosome—the X-shaped structure that contains genetic information inside cells. "That's exactly what I saw, a little X," Iqbal says. The genetics lab also had full-grown sheep in it. "It was amazing! I wanted to know how that little X turned into a sheep."

Later Iqbal went to university to study biology. After many years of studying, he had the chance to work on a research project to learn more about the infectious disease known as HIV/AIDS. His mission was to figure out why some women in Africa seemed to fight off this disease and not get sick from it, even though they were exposed to the virus that causes it. While he did this work, Iqbal lived part of the year in Winnipeg and part of the year in Nairobi.

After finishing the project and getting his PhD degree, Iqbal began working with a pharmaceutical company as a scientist. He loved the fast pace and teamwork in industry, and eventually he worked his way up in different companies to the position he now has as medical director for Moderna Canada. "What I like about being in industry is that we're making medicines that help people all over the world, so it has a tremendous global impact," Iqbal says. One part of his job is to get different groups of people involved in clinical trials for vaccines, including Moderna's COVID-19 vaccine. This is where his experience in Nairobi guides him. "Diseases affect people in different ways," Iqbal says. "We have to involve people from diverse communities, from marginalized communities. They must all be represented."

Using a Messenger

In an earlier chapter I mentioned DNA—the instructions for how an organism looks and functions. DNA has two strands shaped like a twisted ladder inside the command center, or *nucleus*, of every plant and animal cell. Scientists discovered DNA in 1953, but they didn't know how the body "reads" or gets the instructions from the DNA. Then, in 1961, French scientists discovered messenger *RNA*—shortened to mRNA—which is similar to DNA but has only one strand. The mRNA makes a copy of the DNA's instructions and takes the copy out of the nucleus and into a *ribosome*. Ribosomes are the factories in cells for building *proteins*. Proteins have many jobs, such as carrying messages, giving structure to cells and moving things around the body.

Later, scientists learned how to make strands of mRNA in the lab and send the strands into cells to take instructions into ribosomes. The scientists looked for ways to use the lab-made mRNA in vaccines. Then, in 2020, COVID-19 began spreading across the world. The scientists were ready! They had all the ingredients and methods in place to make an mRNA vaccine against the SARS-CoV-2 virus. They discovered that this virus has proteins sticking out of its surface like spikes. These spike proteins were a good target for an mRNA vaccine.

So how do the COVID-19 mRNA vaccines work? They send mRNA into the body with instructions for ribosomes to make the spike proteins. As the spike proteins are made, the immune system detects them, realizes they're unfriendly and makes antibodies against them. Later, if the SARS-CoV-2 virus enters the vaccinated person's body, the immune system is ready. The memory cells quickly recognize the spike proteins on the virus and shut it down before it can multiply too many times and make the person sick.

Spike proteins make a coronavirus look like a crown studded with jewels. The word *corona* means "crown."

DOTTED YETI/SHUTTERSTOCK.COM

A computer illustration of a strand of messenger RNA, or mRNA. An mRNA strand is different from DNA, which has two strands. It's not possible for mRNA to combine with DNA, so mRNA cannot change a person's genetic information.
KATERYNA KON/SCIENCE PHOTO LIBRARY/ GETTY IMAGES

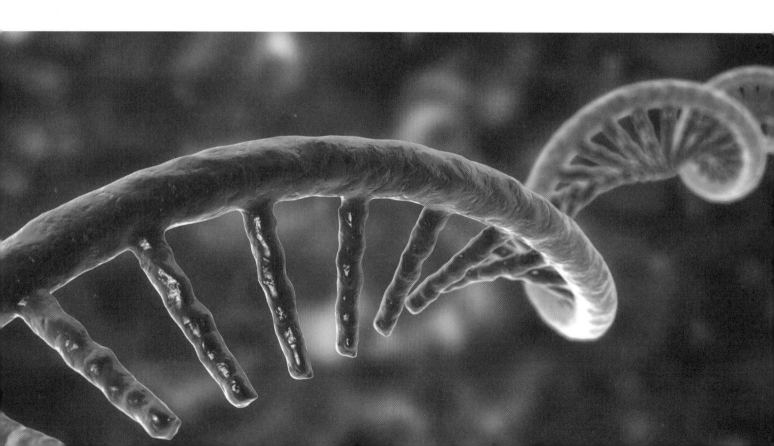

Future
Spreadable Vaccines

SARS-CoV-2 is one of many pathogens that seems to have made an animal-to-human jump, called spillover. Others are the H1N1 influenza, Ebola and Lassa viruses. Would it be possible to stop spillover if we vaccinated animal *populations*? In some countries bats are already vaccinated against rabies to reduce the risk of people getting this deadly disease. But catching and vaccinating wild animals is difficult, time-consuming and very expensive.

Scientists are researching ways to make a vaccine that could spread from animal to animal. One way could be to wipe a vaccine paste onto the fur of a few animals. Some of the paste would most likely get into their mouths and vaccinate them. The paste would also transfer to the fur or paws of the animals' other family members and vaccinate them too. Another way could be to put the vaccine inside a harmless virus that spreads through a group of animals. As the harmless virus got into each animal, the animal's immune system would detect the vaccine hidden inside the virus and make antibodies. The scientists working on spreadable vaccines have lots to think about and study before testing one in a wild-animal population. What things do you think they should study and understand about spreadable vaccines before testing one in the wild?

Vaccine Delivery

Most vaccines need to be injected. A few can be taken by mouth in drops or a drink, and some can be sprayed into the nose. Scientists are looking for easier ways to deliver vaccines. Some are trying to make edible vaccines using bananas or potatoes, and others are studying skin patches and microneedles that a person can't feel go through their skin. That would be nice!

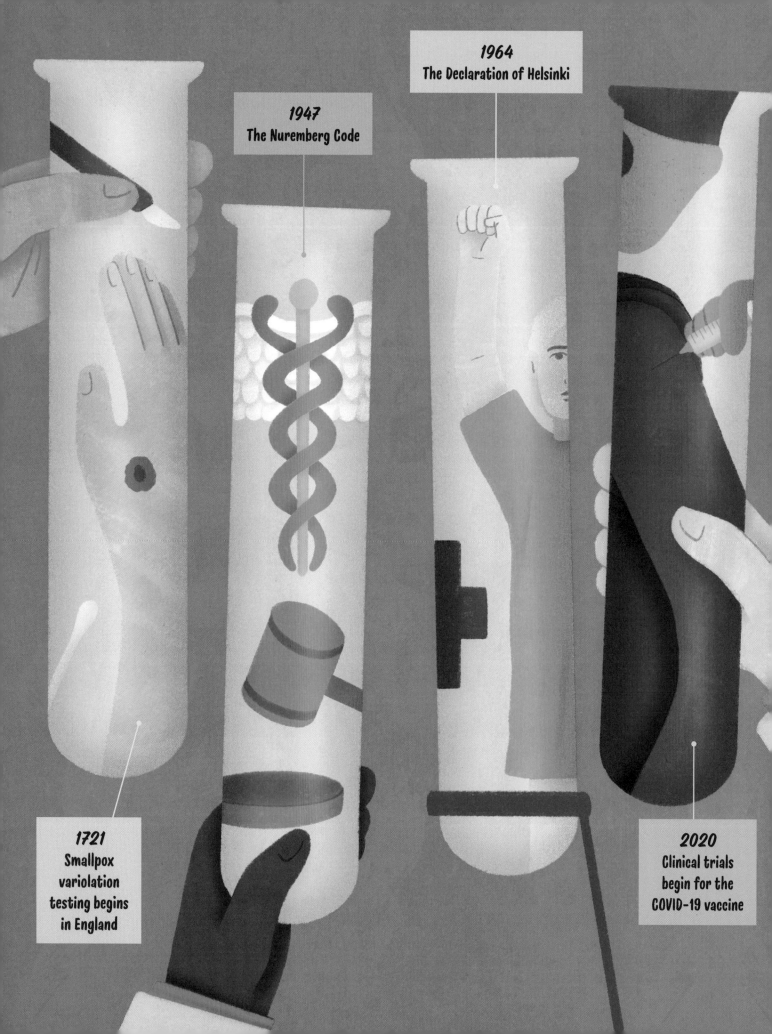

1964
The Declaration of Helsinki

1947
The Nuremberg Code

1721
Smallpox
variolation
testing begins
in England

2020
Clinical trials
begin for the
COVID-19 vaccine

FIVE

TESTING

How to Know If a New Vaccine Works

Do you remember trying something for the first time? Maybe a new activity or going to a new place? Did you feel excited or nervous, or perhaps a bit of both? Without trying new things, you'll never know if you enjoy the activity or like the place.

It's the same with developing a new medication or vaccine. Scientists and doctors don't know whether it will work until they try, or test, it. This is how science works—form a question, then test it. Sometimes a scientist gets a clear answer right away, but more often the test brings up other questions. It can take time and lots of testing to find answers to questions in science. Vaccine testing—also called *clinical trials*—has produced everything from great success to terrible harm. Let's go back to the early days of vaccine discovery to see some examples.

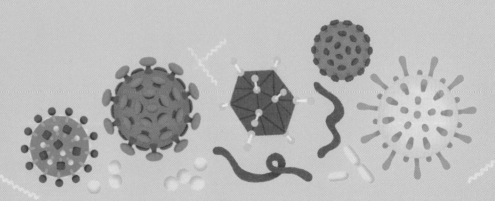

Early Testing

In the early 1700s, Lady Mary Wortley Montagu, wife of an English ambassador, was living in Constantinople, the capital city of the Turkish Ottoman Empire (today it's Istanbul, Turkey). She watched women use the variolation technique of transferring scabs or pus from a sick person to a healthy person to protect them from smallpox. The women used the technique on children in their community, and this fascinated Montagu. She had survived smallpox as a child and been left with scars on her face. Her brother had died from the disease. Now, determined to protect her young son, Montagu had him variolated. She then had the idea to "bring this useful invention into fashion in England," as she wrote to a friend.

A few years later, in 1721, Montagu and her family returned to England, where she asked the embassy doctor,

Charles Maitland, to variolate her young daughter. Afterward Montagu took the little girl into the homes of people with smallpox to show that the child was now protected. This seemingly dangerous act impressed some people, but many others frowned at the foreign variolation technique. So Maitland and a few other doctors planned a test of variolation. They asked King George I to let prisoners at London's Newgate Prison go free if they agreed to be variolated as a test (and if, of course, they survived). The king agreed, and six prisoners were variolated. They not only survived but remained healthy after later exposure to smallpox. All six were freed. The results of this test with prisoners and later tests with orphaned children persuaded many people, including some in the royal family, that variolation was safe.

A portrait of Lady Mary Wortley Montagu, painted by Godfrey Kneller sometime between 1715 and 1720.
YALE CENTER FOR BRITISH ART, PAUL MELLON COLLECTION, PUBLIC DOMAIN

Ethics of Medical Tests

It's heartbreaking to think about the medical testing done on children living in orphanages, prisoners locked up in jail, people with mental illnesses living in institutions and hospital patients too sick to know what was happening to them. It's unethical—not right—to do medical tests in these circumstances. Testing should only be done with people who agree to participate after understanding what the test is for and the possible risks and benefits of participating. This is what it means to give *informed consent*.

In the history of medical testing, many people have been subjected to tests without being asked or even told. This unethical behavior started to change—though slowly—in the early 1900s. After terrible human experiments happened during World War II, several countries worked together in 1947 to write the Nuremberg Code. This code listed what scientists should do before and during a clinical trial, including getting participants' voluntary and informed consent. In 1964 the World Medical Association wrote the Declaration of Helsinki, a set of ethical principles to protect people who participate in clinical trials.

The United States, Canada and many other countries referred to the Nuremberg Code and Declaration of Helsinki as they wrote *laws* about clinical trials and ethical scientific research.

ON THE JOB

Inci Yildirim

"Ask questions. Read to look for answers. Find what you are excited about, and do your best in what you're doing."

Growing up in Turkey, Inci Yildirim and her brother listened to their father's stories at the dinner table. He spoke of his work as a traveling vaccine officer, riding a horse with a cooler on his back. He rode from village to village, giving the villagers vaccines against tuberculosis and polio.

Inspired by her father, Yildirim entered medical school and trained in infectious diseases. As part of this training, she collected samples of spinal fluid from sick children at multiple hospitals around Turkey and analyzed the samples at a lab in England. She discovered that the children were ill with vaccine-preventable diseases. Soon after, a program started to administer the vaccines in Turkey, and the number of cases of these diseases dropped sharply, saving many lives. "This is a justice issue," says Yildirim. "Every child should have the same basic rights and same likelihood to celebrate many birthdays in their future. It shouldn't matter where you are born."

Today Yildirim splits her workdays between caring for young organ-transplant patients who have infections, running clinical trials for vaccines in kids, teaching university students and doing research to help make vaccines more effective for everyone.

During clinical trials, researchers collect a lot of information from trial participants.
FATCAMERA/GETTY IMAGES

Who Participates in Clinical Trials?

Clinical trials rely on volunteers who give their informed consent to participate. People volunteer for clinical trials for many different reasons. For people living with a rare health condition, it may be a chance to get a promising new treatment more quickly. Other people volunteer because they're interested in medicine and science and want to contribute to improving healthcare. Often trials pay volunteers to compensate them for the time and money they spend going to appointments or completing the study requirements.

1900s–Today
Testing in Steps

It takes a lot of steps to make a vaccine, test it and get it approved for use. First comes all the research to develop a possible vaccine—called a *vaccine candidate*. Then scientists test it in animals, often mice and monkeys. Finally, once the vaccine candidate is known to be safe and effective in other animals, tests begin in people to study safety and effectiveness. Clinical trials have three phases:

Phase 1—Testing the vaccine candidate on a very small group of people—sometimes as few as 20—to find out how their immune systems respond and whether the vaccine has any serious side effects.

Phase 2—Testing several hundred people to figure out the best dose of the vaccine and keep studying side effects.

Phase 3—Testing thousands of people to compare vaccinated with unvaccinated people and to look for rare side effects.

Finally, if the results are good, a vaccine developer can apply to the government for a license to make the vaccine available to the public.

These steps can take many years to complete—and they require a lot of money. Many vaccine candidates never make it through the full set of steps to be approved for use. And even once a vaccine is approved, doctors, scientists and vaccine makers keep collecting data to track the vaccine's safety and effectiveness.

Today

The COVID-19 Vaccine

The speed with which COVID-19 vaccines were developed and approved took many people by surprise. Previously it had taken years and years to make a new vaccine. From discovering the pathogen to having a vaccine took more than a century for typhoid fever, four decades for whooping cough and nine years for measles. But it took just under 12 months for COVID-19. Wow!

Several things helped. Money poured in to fund research labs and run tests, with a lot of effort focused on developing a vaccine with existing mRNA technology. Thousands of scientists from all around the world worked together and shared their data. And then, when candidate vaccines were ready, scientists needed to test them on people who would be exposed to COVID-19 after a trial vaccination. With a pandemic underway, this wasn't a problem. It didn't take long to figure out how well the vaccines worked.

There's a big difference in the death rate from COVID-19 for people in the United States who are vaccinated and those who aren't.

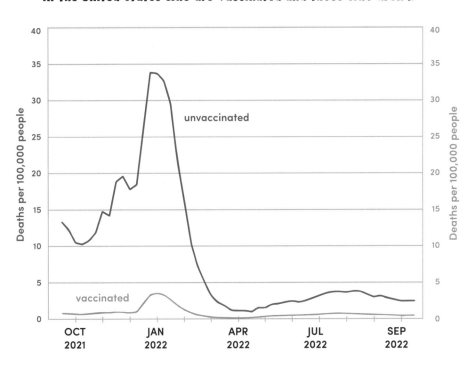

At the peak in January 2022—when the Omicron variant of COVID-19 was circulating—nearly 35 of every 100,000 unvaccinated people died. By comparison, only about 4 of every 100,000 vaccinated people died. This data is from people of all ages in 24 US jurisdictions and represents half of the US population.

CENTERS FOR DISEASE CONTROL AND PREVENTION. COVID DATA TRACKER.
ATLANTA, GA: US DEPARTMENT OF HEALTH AND HUMAN SERVICES, CDC; 2023, MARCH 05.
COVID.CDC.GOV/COVID-DATA-TRACKER/#RATES-BY-VACCINE-STATUS

Safety Tracking

Keeping track of possible side effects from vaccines is really important. Clinical trials focus on safety, but if a side effect is rare, it may not be noticed until the vaccine has been given to hundreds of thousands or even millions of people. Many countries have a vaccine-safety tracking system for doctors and the public to report symptoms that start soon after a person gets vaccinated. If similar reports start coming in from multiple people, public health workers can quickly spot the pattern and look into it.

For example, scientists developed the RotaShield vaccine to prevent sickness from rotavirus, a nasty stomach bug that causes vomiting and diarrhea. But after vaccination, some babies got a rare condition in which a portion of the intestine (the muscular tube between the stomach and anus) folds over on itself. This is painful, and usually it's a medical emergency. In July 1999 the United States' safety tracking system received 15 reports of babies with folded intestines soon after getting RotaShield vaccine. Public health workers investigated and found that the vaccine had caused these cases. Doctors and nurses stopped using the vaccine. The safety tracker had worked as the warning system it's designed to be.

Like all scientific research, vaccine development requires scientists to pay attention to details and make careful, precise measurements in their lab work.
TOM WERNER/GETTY IMAGES

Future
A 100-Day Vaccine

The Coalition for Epidemic Preparedness Innovations, also called CEPI, wants to get the world ready to respond even more quickly than it did for COVID-19 when the next pathogen emerges and threatens to cause a pandemic. If the plan works, the world will go from discovering the Disease X pathogen to vaccinating the public against it in just 100 days!

Here's CEPI's plan:

- Get better at watching for and tracking new pathogens.

- Develop a "vaccine library" with starter vaccines for each of the approximately 25 virus families known to infect humans.

- Prepare testing centers and enroll people in advance for clinical trials so vaccine testing can start quickly.

Do you think CEPI's plan for developing a 100-day vaccine could work?

Being part of a team that develops vaccines is both exciting and rewarding.
SIRO RODENAS CORTES/GETTY IMAGES

ON THE JOB

Tatiana Arias

FERNANDO CONCEIÇÃO

"In biomedical work, the possibilities are wide. There are so many different paths you can take."

When Tatiana Arias was little, her mother predicted she would become a doctor. Sure enough, after high school Arias entered medical school in her hometown of Mexico City. Early in her medical training, she was selected to join a small group of students doing medical-lab research at the same time as studying to become a doctor. Arias's father was a research scientist, so she jumped at the opportunity to follow in his footsteps. For her research project, she tested new vaccines in rats, and this experience changed the direction of her career. Arias finished her medical degree, and instead of working with patients in a clinic or hospital, she took a job with a biomedical company. Biomedical companies develop and test medical products—devices like heart pacemakers and artificial knee joints, medications and vaccines. Today Arias oversees teams of people who run clinical trials to test new vaccines and other products. "I like to organize and make things happen," Arias says. "I'm part of a big chain that makes a product available to people to make their lives better. I feel useful. I feel like I'm making a difference."

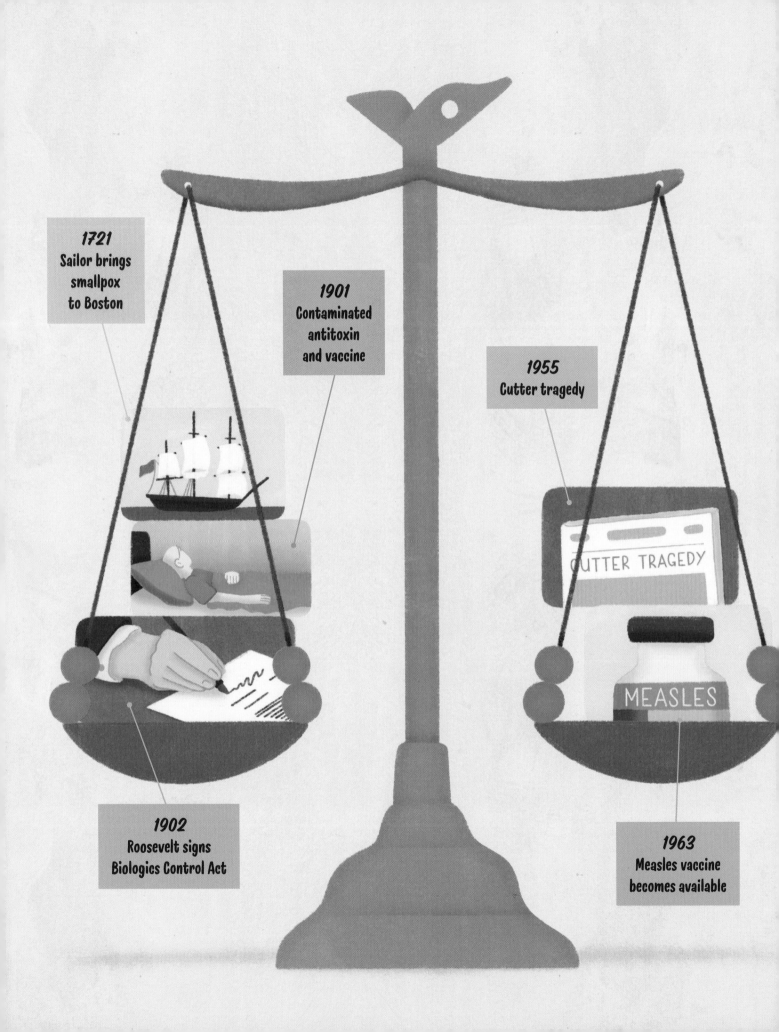

1721
Sailor brings
smallpox
to Boston

1901
Contaminated
antitoxin
and vaccine

1955
Cutter tragedy

CUTTER TRAGEDY

MEASLES

1902
Roosevelt signs
Biologics Control Act

1963
Measles vaccine
becomes available

SIX

RISK

What It Means to Be Vaccinated

What risky things did you do today? Did you play a sport? Or eat an apple? Or watch a screen for hours? Each activity involves risks, although the level of risk differs for each one. A lot of the time, we don't think much before doing an activity, but if there's a high risk of getting hurt, we think more carefully. The critical thing is to weigh the risks of the activity against the benefits. Are the risks small enough? Are the benefits big enough?

Getting a vaccine has risks too. No vaccine is 100 percent risk-free, just like no activity is 100 percent risk-free. In the case of vaccines, the risk is side effects, and the benefit is protection from getting a particular disease. It's a lot to think about! Let's take a look at how people have viewed vaccine risks in the past.

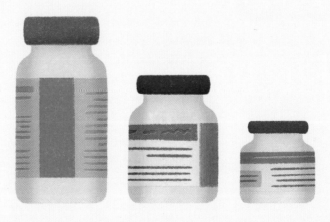

1721

Collecting Data

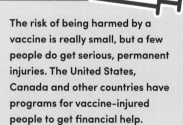

The risk of being harmed by a vaccine is really small, but a few people do get serious, permanent injuries. The United States, Canada and other countries have programs for vaccine-injured people to get financial help.

Cotton Mather was a Puritan minister in Boston. Like many colonists at the time, he had slaves who worked in his home. One of them, a man called Onesimus, told Mather how he had been variolated as a boy in Africa to protect him from smallpox. Intrigued, Mather talked with other African slaves and learned what he could about the technique. He became convinced that variolation would save lives in his hometown of Boston.

When a sailor brought smallpox to the city in 1721 and the virus spread, Mather urged local doctors to variolate Bostonians. Only one doctor, Zabdiel Boylston, stepped forward to help. He began variolating people, and—importantly for this story—he and Mather kept records. By the end of the Boston smallpox outbreak several months later, 5,759 Bostonians had caught smallpox, and 844 of them had died. That means 14.6 percent of the infected people died. Boylston and Mather's records showed that Boylston variolated 247 people and six of them died—that's 2.4 percent. Looking at those numbers, people could see the lower risk of death from having variolation than from getting natural smallpox. Variolation held risks, but the benefits outweighed the risks. Boylston and Mather's data helped to persuade more people to get variolated.

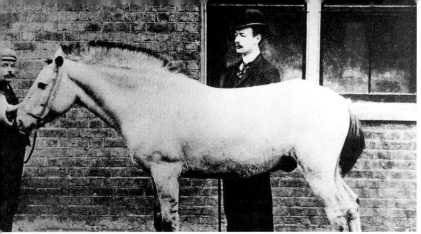

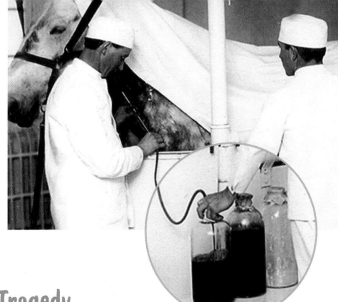

Horses injected with diphtheria toxin have an immune response that builds up an antitoxin in their blood. After the blood has been collected in bottles, it can then be purified to make an antitoxin medicine to use in people. The first horse used, seen here on the left, was in England in 1894. (LEFT) WIKIMEDIA COMMONS/WELLCOME IMAGES/CC BY 4.0; (RIGHT) WIKIMEDIA COMMONS/NATIONAL ARCHIVES AND RECORDS ADMINISTRATION/PUBLIC DOMAIN

1901

Twenty-two Children

Two disasters happened in 1901, both because of contamination. In October a doctor visited the home of Bessie Baker, a little girl who was sick with a bacterial disease called diphtheria. The doctor gave Bessie the standard treatment—an *antitoxin* that works against the part of diphtheria that causes illness. This treatment was usually very effective, but Bessie got worse. It turned out she had contracted another illness, called tetanus. The diphtheria antitoxin the doctor had given her was contaminated with live tetanus bacteria. Sadly, Bessie and 12 other children in St. Louis, Missouri, died from this batch of contaminated antitoxin.

A month later a second disaster happened when nine children died from tetanus bacteria. These children had received a contaminated smallpox vaccine in Camden, New Jersey. In 1901 the United States had no standards for the production of medicines and vaccines. Anybody could make and sell them. Something clearly had to change. Within a year of these 22 children's deaths, then-president Theodore Roosevelt signed a law called the Biologics Control Act. It was the first US law to control the purity of vaccines and antitoxins. With this control in place, the risk of contaminated medicines and vaccines went down.

1955

The Cutter Tragedy

As you read in chapter 4, polio was a terrible disease that caused widespread fear in the 1950s. Unfortunately, during the race to develop a polio vaccine, another devastating incident happened. In 1954, clinical trials of the killed-polio vaccine included more than 1.5 million children in the United States, Canada and Finland. The trials showed that the vaccine was safe and very effective against polio. The next step was to vaccinate as many people as possible. So five vaccine makers were chosen to produce the vaccine. As one of them, Cutter Laboratories, followed the instructions to make the vaccine, something went wrong. One batch of vaccine mistakenly had full-strength poliovirus in it. Cutter Labs realized the mistake and made an urgent announcement, but it was too late—380,000 doses of the bad batch had already been given to children. More than half of them got sick with polio, 164 became paralyzed and 10 died from polio as a result of the ill-fated batch of vaccine.

This tragedy made it clear that vaccine production needed much better safety controls. Today we have safe vaccines with very, very low risk because the children affected by the Cutter tragedy and earlier disasters paid such a high price.

Effectiveness Varies

No vaccine works 100 percent of the time. A vaccine's effectiveness at preventing sickness depends on the type of vaccine and the person getting the vaccine. A 12-year-old who gets a flu vaccine will be better protected against flu than an 80-year-old. That's because the younger person's immune system is stronger and can respond better to the vaccine. Even so, the 80-year-old still gets some protection from the vaccine and is less likely to get a really bad case of flu or die from it.

What are the chances that you will...

...get sick from food poisoning in any given year?

1 in 6

...be struck by lightning in your lifetime?

1 in 15,300

...die from a hornet, wasp or bee sting in your lifetime?

1 in 54,500

...be able to guess, in the right order, the last five digits of this book author's phone number?

1 in 100,500

...experience anaphylaxis from a vaccination?

1 in 1 million

* to be truly to scale with the other four dots, this blue dot should be as wide as an NBA basketball court!

DATA FROM THE CDC, NATIONAL WEATHER SERVICE, NATIONAL SAFETY COUNCIL AND *JOURNAL OF ALLERGY AND CLINICAL IMMUNOLOGY*, 137:868–878, 2016

The Risk of Not Getting Vaccinated

The flip side to the very small risk that comes with getting vaccinated is the very high risk that comes with *not* getting vaccinated. Said differently, vaccines have low risks and provide high benefits. Throughout this book, you're reading about the benefits of vaccination in preventing disabling and often deadly infectious diseases. These benefits are easy to see when you look at the number of people who got sick from a particular disease before and after a vaccine was available. Measles cases in the United States make a great example. Before the measles vaccine, about 500,000 cases of the illness were reported each year. Within only a few years of the measles vaccine becoming available in 1963, cases began to decline. Recent data from the Centers for Disease Control and Prevention show that from 2010 to 2022, an average of 263 people had measles each year in the United States.

Today

Vaccine Side Effects

Vaccine side effects typically include soreness, redness or swelling at the injection site, muscle aches, headache, mild fever and tiredness. They show that your immune system is doing its job of building immunity to the disease. These side effects usually go away within a few days.

Vaccines also have a very small risk of causing a serious allergic reaction called **anaphylaxis** (pronounced ana-FIH-lax-us). This reaction starts soon after the vaccine enters the body. That's why the nurse asks you to stay at the health clinic for 15 minutes after getting vaccinated. People who experience anaphylaxis have trouble breathing and often get an itchy rash, a racing heart and swollen lips or tongue. This is clearly very, very scary, but it's treatable with immediate medical care.

What is the chance of anaphylaxis happening? Extremely small. So small that it's hard to write it down: 0.0000013 percent. Written a different way, for every one million vaccine doses given, about one person will experience anaphylaxis.

Future
Think about It

To be alive is to live with risks. It's impossible to get away from risks. There will be new infectious diseases that come along, and old ones might return. There will be new vaccines developed and probably also new techniques for understanding pathogens and creating vaccines against them. If we use critical thinking skills and accurate information from experts, we can make good decisions that keep many risks low.

Important parts of critical thinking:

- Be curious and ask questions.
- Keep an open mind.
- Look for relevant information from experts.
- Evaluate the sources of information you find.
- Analyze the information you find.

Do you think enough people will understand the value of critical thinking—and use it to evaluate risks—in the future?

ON THE JOB

Mallory Bergum

MALLORY BERGUM

Mallory Bergum got her introduction to healthcare while she worked at a front desk admitting patients to a busy emergency room in Vancouver, BC. She saw the nurses working with patients and decided she wanted to be one of them. Bergum went to university and graduated with a nursing degree just as the COVID-19 pandemic was declared. So for her first job, she cared for patients on a COVID unit.

Her next move took her north—way north to Dawson City, a town of about 1,500 people in Yukon, on the Traditional Territories of the Tr'ondëk Hwëch'in First Nation. There Bergum is one of two community health nurses who do everything from checking babies to caring for people with chronic (long-term) conditions to giving vaccines.

"The variety in nursing is huge. There are so many different fields, different types of nursing. You'll never be bored!"

1885
Montreal Vaccine Riot

1998
False info is spread about the MMR vaccine

FALSE

92%

2018
Survey shows people agree vaccines for children are important

2020s
Celebrities spread misinformation

SEVEN

RELUCTANCE

When People Hesitate about Vaccines

Because of vaccination, fewer people die today or live with lifelong problems from infectious diseases than decades ago. Smallpox no longer exists, and another disease—polio—is close to being wiped out. Yet more than 1.5 million people still die every year from diseases that can be prevented with vaccines. Why?

There are two reasons. One, for some people it's difficult to get vaccines. Unequal access to vaccines is the subject of a later chapter. Two, some people doubt the effectiveness or safety of vaccines. These people are vaccine hesitant. They put off getting a vaccine or decide not to get vaccinated even though vaccination clinics are available to them. People of all genders, ages and backgrounds may be vaccine hesitant. Typically, vaccine-hesitant people want to make the best decision for their own and their children's health. But it can be hard to filter accurate, scientific information about vaccines from the widespread false information about them that is also out there.

> The World Health Organization made a list in 2019 of the top 10 threats to global health. One of the 10 was vaccine hesitancy.

1885
Rioting in Montreal

In March 1885 a train arrived in Montreal. One of the train conductors had smallpox virus, and soon it was spreading through the city. Thousands of people became sick. At the end of September, public health workers announced mandatory smallpox vaccination—that is, the government told people they *had* to get vaccinated. A lot of angry people swarmed around the public health department's office building and smashed windows of drugstores and the police station headquarters. This was the Montreal Vaccine Riot.

Anti-vaccine protests happened in other places too, and the protesters formed groups, such as the Anti-Vaccination Society of America, to promote their messages. The people against vaccines had several different reasons. Some of them objected to the government trying to take away their personal freedoms. Others thought it was wrong to meddle in the fate God gave each person. And a lot of people were afraid—they didn't trust that the vaccine worked or was safe.

Mental Mistakes

Numbers can show us the risks associated with different activities and events, but not everybody examines the numbers when deciding how to act. Or should I say, not every *brain* examines the numbers. Our brains use mental shortcuts to make decisions in day-to-day life. Many of these shortcuts draw on our past experiences. Say you and a friend decide to go for ice cream. Your mom says a new place has opened nearby. You usually go to the place across town, so you go back there instead of trying the new place. This is the "familiarity" mental shortcut at work—you made a decision based on being familiar with the place across town. There are more than a dozen mental shortcuts. They speed up our everyday decisions, but they can also lead us to make mistakes when we rely on them for important decisions, such as getting vaccinated.

Imagine this scenario. You know three people who recently got sick with COVID-19. They all had mild symptoms and were back to their regular activities after a few days. You conclude that COVID isn't that bad, and you decide not to get vaccinated. You've used the "availability" mental shortcut—you made a decision based on available information that came easily to mind. But you could have made a more informed decision by considering other information, such as how many people in your community got COVID-19, how severe their symptoms were, whether any of them died and whether those who were vaccinated had less severe illness than those who were unvaccinated. With the mental shortcut, you made an easy, fast decision, but it used only a fraction of the available information.

1998

The Far Reach of Fraud

In 1998 an English doctor published an article in a respected medical journal. He described a link between autism in children and the MMR vaccine (a combination vaccine that protects against measles, mumps and rubella). The media picked up the story, and headlines screamed the news. But it turned out that his research study had many things wrong with it. And on top of this, he had been paid to find evidence of a link. When this information surfaced, the British medical council took away the man's license, so he could no longer treat patients, and the medical journal withdrew the article.

But by the time the truth came out, it was already too late. Alarmed parents all over the world refused to let their children get the MMR vaccine. Even today, more than 25 years later and after dozens of other research studies have tested the

vaccine and concluded that it is safe, the discredited idea still exists. This is called *misinformation*. Purposely spreading discredited or false information, such as the idea about the MMR vaccine, is called *disinformation*. When it comes to vaccines, some people use disinformation to try to influence other people's behavior. Maybe they're selling products in place of vaccines. Maybe they don't want to get vaccinated, and they want others to agree with their point of view. Maybe they don't trust the government or science, and they want to sow distrust among others. People can have many reasons for intentionally spreading false information, which is why it's so important to always evaluate information critically.

The first page of *The Lancet* medical journal article published in 1998 with false information about the MMR vaccine. The journal later withdrew, or retracted, the article, meaning that it is no longer part of the scientific record.

Learn as much science as you can at school, and explore nature as much as possible too! No matter what career you want to have—whether in science or not—your life will always be affected by science. So the more science you know and understand, the better you can navigate life to keep yourself (and our planet) safe and healthy.

Today
Trust in Science

Our entire world is built on science. All the plants, animals and people on Earth are marvels of biology. We live on a planet that displays powerful shows of geology through earthquakes and volcanic eruptions. We experience meteorology daily in the weather. We use physics every time we ride on a bicycle or in a vehicle, and chemistry every time we cook food.

Despite all the evidence of science around us, some people don't trust science or scientists. This distrust comes from many places, including not understanding how science works. A scientist asks a question, forms a *hypothesis* and then collects data to test the hypothesis. If the data show the hypothesis is incorrect, the scientist forms a new hypothesis and collects new data. Scientific studies sometimes contradict each other, so other scientists design new ways to test a hypothesis and collect more data. Science progresses like this in small steps—some forward, some backward—and over time there's so much data to support a particular hypothesis that most scientists agree with it. But a few people misunderstand the back-and-forth steps and the contradictory studies. They become suspicious of science and don't trust information coming from scientists, whether it's about climate change, genetically modified foods or vaccines.

When I was the age of this child, I had never heard of a computer! I looked in library books and encyclopedias to find information for school projects. Now you and I can use the internet to find lots of information, both accurate and false.
CARLOS BARQUERO/GETTY IMAGES

Doing Your Own Information "Research"

Type a few words into an internet search engine, click a button and poof! Pages and pages of information appear on your screen. The internet and social media have totally changed how we learn about things, where we get information and from whom we get it. Some people view internet searches as "research," but scientific research is very different from internet research. When we search for information or see it on social media, we need to keep a few things in mind:

Anyone can say nearly anything they want, and other people will read it. This is both exciting and dangerous. It's exciting because there's a lot of interesting and accurate information out there. And it's dangerous because there's also a lot of false and deceptive information out there. Telling one from the other takes time and thought.

Journalists and their editors and fact-checkers used to be the gatekeepers of information published in printed newspapers and magazines. Even though some of these news sources still exist (often online instead of in print), many people now get their news and information from social media—where there aren't fact-checkers.

A lot of content on social media is visual, such as photos, videos and memes. People typically take in visual information more quickly than text, and they often accept it as true without questioning it. Visual information needs to be fact-checked as much as text-based information does.

Some famous people abuse their fame by sharing information on topics they have no knowledge about—like infectious diseases and vaccines. These celebrities are sharing their *opinions*, but sometimes it sounds like expert information. It's okay to follow celebrities, but follow them for what they do best—acting, singing, playing sports. And get information about health and science from the people who trained in and know these subjects the best—scientists, researchers, doctors and other healthcare workers.

Young Anna Argyris

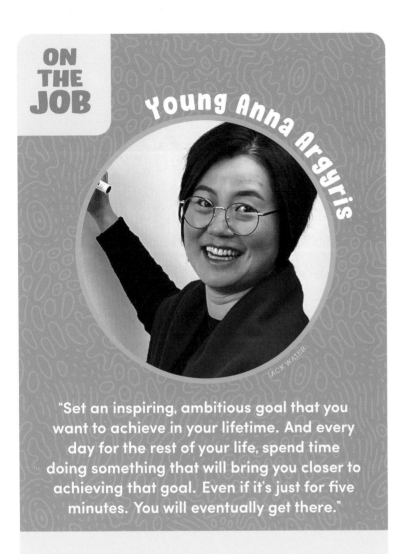

JACK WAIER

"Set an inspiring, ambitious goal that you want to achieve in your lifetime. And every day for the rest of your life, spend time doing something that will bring you closer to achieving that goal. Even if it's just for five minutes. You will eventually get there."

When she's at work, Young Anna Argyris thinks a lot about social media posts—and especially about all the vaccine misinformation she sees in posts. "Many educated parents believe anti-vaccine information," she says. "But why?"

Argyris uses her education and experience in information systems to look for answers. At the moment she is working on two projects. In the first, she is aiming to understand the personal beliefs of vaccine-hesitant people. How have they formed these beliefs against vaccines? And for the second project, she is studying the things that popular anti-vaccine posts on social media have in common. How are they written, and what words are used in the posts that get shared widely?

Argyris plans to use the results of these two projects to create a chatbot to address misinformed vaccine beliefs and give accurate information about vaccines. "So much information is generated each day. The possibilities are endless," says Argyris.

Future
Techno Tools

It's hard to understand why some people give out false information on purpose. One way to keep away from it on the internet is not to see it in the first place. For this, information technology itself may be able to come to the rescue. For example, media and information researchers have started creating tools that plug into an internet browser and work as a kind of fact-checker. These browser tools can pop up warning messages to help people sort accurate health information from false information.

As well as using technology tools, we can all help stop the spread of false information. We must evaluate what we read and hear and be careful about what we say and share, both online and offline. Forwarding or reposting something you haven't fact-checked or evaluated carefully can cause you to accidentally spread bad information.

Can you think of other ways to help stop the spread of false information?

EVALUATING INTERNET (AND OTHER) SOURCES

Use the **5 Ws** to evaluate an information source:

WHO is the author?

WHAT is their background or expertise?

WHERE do they work or what organization are they linked with?

WHY are they writing or giving out this information?

WHEN did they write or prepare the information?

Laws

1855
Massachusetts schools require vaccines

NO VACCINE, NO SCHOOL

1905
Vaccine laws created for the "common good"

2015
California changes laws for certain childhood vaccination exemptions

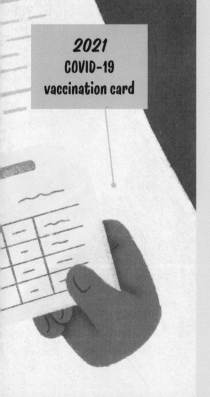

2021
COVID-19
vaccination card

RULES

When Vaccines Are Required

Does your family have rules? Maybe you have to take your shoes off at the door, or keep your elbows off the dinner table. Every family has different rules, and so do countries, states and cities. They have rules—called laws—telling people what they must do and what they must not do. Some laws are easy to understand. You must wear a seat belt in a moving vehicle. You must not steal from other people. Other laws aren't as easy to figure out—like for vaccines. Should there be a law saying that people must get vaccinated?

Here's the thing. A vaccine protects one person from getting a particular disease, but it also protects their entire community. How? When most people are vaccinated—usually 80 to 95 percent of the population, depending on the disease—then even an unvaccinated person can be protected from getting sick. This is because the pathogen won't be able to find enough hosts (unvaccinated people) to live in and spread between. Called ***herd immunity*** (or community immunity), this effect is a lifeline for people who can't have a particular vaccine for medical reasons and for babies too young to start getting vaccines. Also, people having cancer treatments or preparing for an organ transplant have weakened immune systems and aren't as well protected by vaccines as healthy people are. So should everyone who's healthy enough and old enough to get a vaccine be required to have it? This is a tough question and one that people have been asking since the 1800s.

How does herd immunity work?

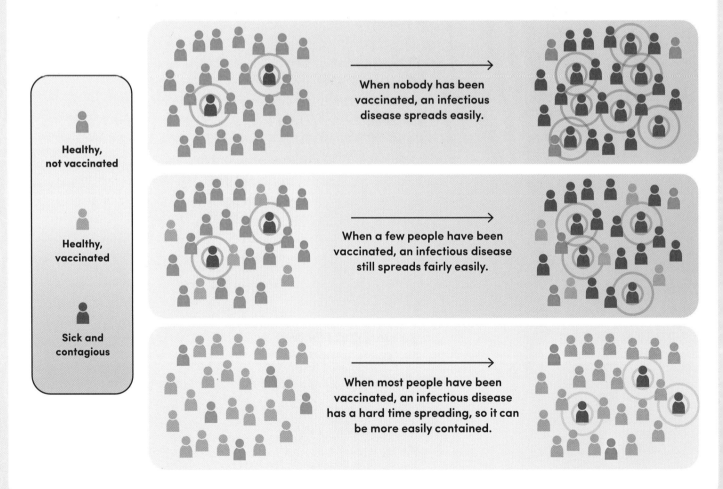

Healthy, not vaccinated

Healthy, vaccinated

Sick and contagious

When nobody has been vaccinated, an infectious disease spreads easily.

When a few people have been vaccinated, an infectious disease still spreads fairly easily.

When most people have been vaccinated, an infectious disease has a hard time spreading, so it can be more easily contained.

1855

Requiring the Smallpox Vaccine

After Edward Jenner's vaccine tests to keep people safe from smallpox, vaccination spread across Europe and North America. Soon governments got involved by making laws that said certain people had to get the smallpox vaccine.

Massachusetts was the first state to say that all children had to go to school. But health workers realized that having all children attend school meant smallpox could easily spread among the students, then to their families and others in the community. So, starting in 1855, children in Massachusetts had to be vaccinated against smallpox to attend public school. More states started making similar laws, and so did governments in other countries.

Vaccine laws vary around the world. Some places, such as many South American, European and Middle Eastern countries, require all children to be vaccinated against certain diseases. Other countries, including the United States and Germany, require certain childhood vaccines for children to enter school. Still others, such as Canada, Australia and Japan, recommend childhood vaccinations but don't require them.

Going to Court

Another law in the state of Massachusetts said that the government could require adults to get the smallpox vaccine if an outbreak started. In 1902 smallpox broke out in the city of Cambridge, near Boston. Most people got the vaccine, but a man named Henning Jacobson refused. He wanted control over what went into his body. He also refused to pay the $5 fine for not getting vaccinated (today that would be about $175). Instead he went to court to protest the law.

Jacobson lost his case in local court and appealed to the Supreme Court of the United States. Jacobson's appeal was heard in 1905, and he lost that case too. By a vote of 7–2, the Supreme Court ruled that governments make laws for the "common good," so to protect public health during a disease outbreak, they can require vaccination. According to this ruling, which still holds today, the rights of a whole community outweigh the rights of an individual.

Seeking an Exemption

Many places allow exemptions from being vaccinated for specific reasons. Some people have legitimate medical reasons why they can't be vaccinated at all or can't have certain vaccines. These people can get a medical exemption from vaccination. Others seek an exemption because they don't want some or all vaccines for philosophical (personal belief) or religious reasons. Many religious leaders disagree with religious exemptions from vaccination. Some have also spoken publicly about their support for vaccines. For example, in 2021, Pope Francis recorded a video address in which he said, "Thanks to God's grace and to the work of many, we now have vaccines to protect us from COVID-19. They bring hope to end the pandemic, but only if they are available to all and if we collaborate with one another. Getting the vaccines that are authorized by the respective authorities is an act of love."

Pharmacists have a wealth of information about medicines and also about vaccines.
MORSA IMAGES/GETTY IMAGES

2014–2015
Catching a Ride

In late 2014 and early 2015, unvaccinated visitors to Disneyland in California got more than selfies with Mickey Mouse. They got measles. More than 150 people became ill with this highly contagious disease. Because many Disneyland visitors came from elsewhere, the measles outbreak spread to other states and to Mexico and Canada. It turned out that about one of every three schoolchildren in California lived in an area with low vaccination rates, so this outbreak spread quite easily. As a result, the government of California changed the laws to stop allowing philosophical and religious exemptions for childhood vaccinations. Some parents resisted, but within two years vaccination rates were back up to the 95 percent level needed for herd immunity.

ON THE JOB

Brendan Parent

NYU LANGONE HEALTH

"Explore. Try new things to discover what makes you tick."

Brendan Parent's path after high school included fixing motorbikes, writing a novel and completing two university degrees—one in bioethics and the second in law. Then he landed a job as a medical ethicist. "I get paid to think about what we should do in challenging situations," he says.

On any given day, Parent might be at his computer writing an article, in a boardroom giving advice to a company CEO on a vaccine policy for staff or in a hospital intensive care unit helping family members decide the fate of their critically ill relative. "I try not to recommend what they do," he says. "I talk about what's at stake, the consequences and what will lead to the most just outcomes. I prefer to help them come to their own decisions."

Parent sees more and more opportunities coming up for medical ethicists. "There are lots of issues to think about," he says. These issues include:

- Big data, artificial intelligence and what they mean for access to healthcare
- Gender-affirming care and how to support people in their preferred identity
- Access for vulnerable populations to preventive care, such as vaccines

2021–Today

Dealing with a Pandemic

Even though the *Jacobson v Massachusetts* ruling happened over 100 years ago, it got talked about when COVID-19 vaccines started getting approved. Many countries, states, provinces, territories and other places made COVID vaccine *mandates*—rules put in place quickly to deal with a particular situation. Some of these vaccine mandates applied to everyone, others to particular groups or activities. For example, where I live in British Columbia, everyone who wanted to eat in a restaurant or go to a public event had to show their vaccine card—proof that they'd had the required vaccine doses.

Some governments added punishments to their vaccine mandates. In Greece and Italy, for example, older adults were fined about $100 if they weren't vaccinated. And in Singapore, unvaccinated people who needed medical care for a COVID-19 infection had to pay for the care themselves. Even with vaccine mandates, some people resisted vaccination. Many who didn't agree with the mandates were very vocal about it. For three weeks in 2022, protesters occupied the downtown streets of Canada's capital city, Ottawa, demanding that the government remove its COVID-19 vaccine mandates.

Mandatory or Voluntary?

Most ethics and public health researchers agree that instead of making vaccines mandatory, it's better to educate people and provide easy access to vaccines so that people will get vaccinated voluntarily. But what should governments do when too few people voluntarily get themselves and their children vaccinated to keep the population in the herd-immunity zone? This is when governments may decide to make vaccine laws or mandates. Making vaccination mandatory does increase the number of people who get vaccinated, but some researchers are concerned that it also pushes certain people to dig in their heels about not getting vaccinated and might make some people less trusting of the government.

Another tactic is to offer money or prizes as incentives for people to get vaccinated. During the COVID-19 pandemic, some governments and organizations gave out cash, others ran lotteries for prizes and some provided food, such as free eggs in Beijing and hummus in Tel Aviv. Incentives can persuade more people to get vaccinated, but often not a large percentage of the population.

What do you think is the best approach to achieving herd immunity in a population of people?

In many parts of the world, restaurants and other public gathering places required people to show they had been vaccinated against COVID-19 before they could enter.
SANYASM/GETTY IMAGES

Receiving an Organ Transplant

In a few cases, people who refused to get the COVID vaccine lost their place in line for an organ transplant, and others weren't allowed to get on the waiting list. When a person receives a transplanted organ, they must take medication to hold back, or suppress, their immune system so their body doesn't attack the new organ. But a suppressed immune system makes the transplant patient extremely vulnerable to infectious diseases. Since there aren't enough transplant organs for everyone who needs one, doctors who do these surgeries want their patients to have the best possible chance of surviving—which means getting vaccinated against several infectious diseases. The ethical question that came up was this: If someone won't accept a life-saving preventive measure like a vaccine, do they have the right to receive a life-prolonging organ that is in short supply when they might not live as long with the new organ as someone else on the transplant list who is willing to have the vaccine?

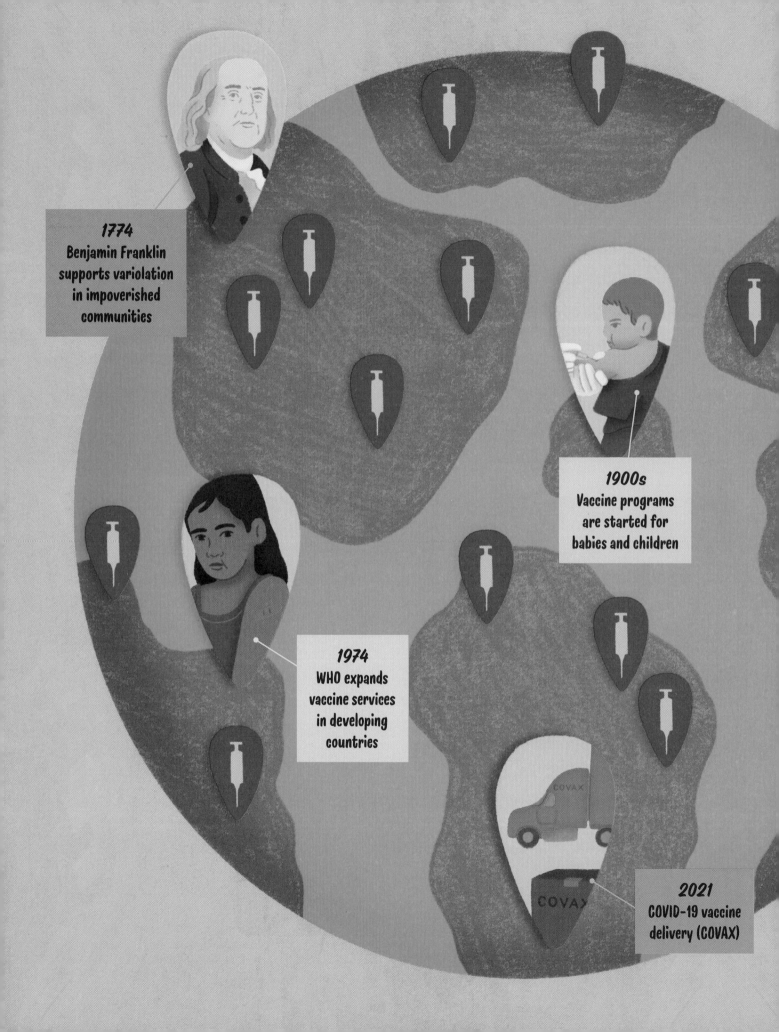

1774
Benjamin Franklin
supports variolation
in impoverished
communities

1900s
Vaccine programs
are started for
babies and children

1974
WHO expands
vaccine services
in developing
countries

2021
COVID-19 vaccine
delivery (COVAX)

NINE

ACCESS

How Vaccines Get Distributed

Do you have a sibling, cousin or friend who has something you don't have? Something you wish you had? I bet it feels unfair. Much of what we have as we grow up depends on our family's circumstances and where in the world we happened to be born. I'm not talking about toys or electronics or books. I mean safe housing, nutritious food, clean drinking water, proper education and good healthcare—including access to vaccines. These are some of the basic rights that everyone on the planet should have. But not everyone does.

Vaccines aren't easily available to everyone. There's a huge difference between developed countries, like the United States and Canada, and developing countries, like Brazil, India and Uganda. Developed countries have enough money to buy vaccines and help their citizens get vaccinated, but many developing countries can't afford to do this. For example, in 2022 one dose of the COVID-19 vaccine cost up to about US $20 for a developing country with low income. For many low-income countries, this amount is half of the total money spent on healthcare for each of their citizens each year. So giving the recommended two COVID-19 vaccine doses per person would use up *all* the available healthcare money for the year without spending anything on other illnesses or injuries. These differences between developed and developing countries create vaccine inequity around the globe.

Even in developed countries there's unequal access to vaccination. Some people don't get basic vaccines, or they only get some doses, leaving them unprotected or only partially protected from preventable infectious diseases. The people in these situations are often members of communities that experience racism, discrimination or financial hardship.

In 2021 Physicians for Human Rights and other health organizations held a demonstration outside the United Nations headquarters building in New York. They were demanding that COVID-19 vaccines—and other vaccines in the future—be more fairly distributed among *all* countries. Their message was that the world would not be safe from COVID-19 until everyone was safe from it.

BLOOMBERG/GETTY IMAGES

Diseases Don't Discriminate

In November 1736 a boy named Francis ("Franky") died of smallpox just a month after his fourth birthday. Franky was the son of Benjamin Franklin, a famous inventor and scientist and one of the founding fathers of the United States. Franklin was an early believer in the variolation technique, and he had intended for his son to be variolated. But the boy wasn't, and he died. Decades later Franklin wrote in his autobiography:

> I long regretted bitterly, and still regret that I had not given it to him by inoculation [another word for variolation]. This I mention for the sake of parents who omit that operation, on the supposition that they should never forgive themselves if the child died under it, my example showing that the regret may be the same either way, and that, therefore, the safer should be chosen.

Years later Franklin continued to support variolation. With information from a doctor, he wrote and published a pamphlet about variolation and its effectiveness. He urged people to get variolated. Later he started a society to help people living in poverty get variolated for free.

Making Ripples

Vaccinating a child is like dropping a pebble in a pond and making ripples. The vaccine helps not just the child but their family, community and country. When a child is vaccinated to help them stay healthy:

- They miss fewer days of school, so they get a better education, which can later help them get a good job.

- Parents don't need to take as much time off work to care for a sick child, so the family makes more money. Having more money means spending more money, which helps the economy.

- They need fewer visits to health clinics and hospitals, saving money that can be spent in other ways.

Vaccinating adults is important for many of these reasons too. Also, vaccinating women before or during pregnancy means they will pass protective antibodies to their unborn babies. These antibodies help protect babies in the early months of life when they can't yet receive certain vaccines themselves.

Vaccinating the World

As more vaccines were invented during the 1900s, developed countries started vaccine programs for babies and children. Vaccination became a routine part of healthcare for children in the first five years of life. The programs weren't perfect, but they helped more children get vaccinated. By the end of the 1960s, many children in developed countries had protection against a handful of diseases, including whooping cough, diphtheria, polio and measles.

But in the world's developing countries, less than 5 percent of children were being fully vaccinated. Imagine a classroom with 20 students and only one of them is safe from diseases like measles and polio. That classroom is like a developing country.

In 1974 the World Health Organization started a program to create and expand vaccine services so that more children in developing countries had access to basic childhood vaccines. In just 15 years, the percentage of vaccinated children jumped from 5 to 50 percent—equal to 10 of the 20 students in that classroom. Today it's over 80 percent—16 of the 20 students are protected. But those four unvaccinated students remain unprotected. When you expand that imaginary classroom to include all children around the world, those four children represent millions of children who remain at risk of dying or being severely harmed by totally preventable diseases.

Human papillomavirus (HPV) is a common infection that can cause cancers of the mouth, throat, neck, rectum and reproductive organs in men and women. The first HPV vaccine came out in 2005 and is available for youth of age nine and up. It's one of only two vaccines (so far) that protect against cancer. The other is for the hepatitis B virus, which causes liver cancer.

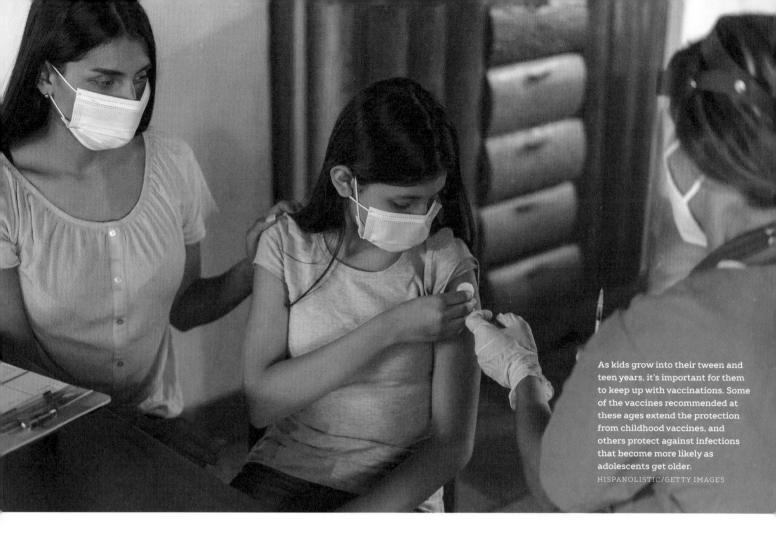

As kids grow into their tween and teen years, it's important for them to keep up with vaccinations. Some of the vaccines recommended at these ages extend the protection from childhood vaccines, and others protect against infections that become more likely as adolescents get older.
HISPANOLISTIC/GETTY IMAGES

2021–Today
No One Is Safe until Everyone Is Safe

When COVID vaccines were first made, there weren't enough to give to everyone. Who should be first in line? Most countries gave priority to healthcare workers, older adults and people with serious health issues. Most developed countries, that is, because developing countries didn't even have vaccine doses at the beginning.

Even once vaccine supply increased, developed countries were giving it to healthy adults and teens while many developing countries had next to nobody vaccinated, not even their healthcare workers. In May 2022, more than a year after the first COVID vaccines rolled out, only 16 percent of people in developing countries had had the first of the two-shot vaccine. In developed countries, more than 80 percent had. The thing is, the longer it takes to vaccinate the world's population, the more chances the SARS-CoV-2 virus has to change its form—*mutate*—into other *variants* and infect more people.

A global partnership called COVAX tried to even out the unequal access. COVAX collected donations of the COVID vaccine from countries with extra doses and sent them to developing countries. This plan worked in part but not as smoothly as hoped, since many of the countries didn't donate as many doses as they originally agreed to.

The COVID-19 pandemic also affected routine vaccinations. When the world went into lockdown to slow the coronavirus's spread, health clinics and other vaccine-delivery programs got turned upside down. As a result, millions of children and adults didn't get their vaccines or got fewer doses than they should have.

69

Prativa Baral

ANNIE VIENS PHOTOGRAPHE

"Don't be afraid to reach out to interesting people and ask them questions."

When she was five, Prativa Baral moved with her family from her birth country of Nepal to Canada. She learned to speak French and English, and she spoke Nepali at home. Speaking this language came in handy when, as a teen, Baral helped Nepali-speaking Bhutanese refugees get settled in their new home—the province of Quebec. These families had been living in camps where healthcare was limited, so some of them had health problems, often from preventable diseases. This experience got Baral thinking about healthcare. "Everyone deserves to have good access to healthcare irrespective of all else. Health is—and should be—a human right."

Baral became an infectious-disease epidemiologist—a scientist who figures out how and why a particular health problem happens in a population of people and what can be done to control the problem or prevent it in the future. Not long after she became an epidemiologist, the COVID-19 pandemic began. Baral leaped into action, using her knowledge to help people understand what was happening. She also began working with the World Bank to keep track of global health systems, and with the World Health Organization to better understand how social conditions, economic factors and environmental issues affect people's health. By understanding these things, Baral says, "we can catch threats to human health early rather than constantly reacting, often late. We need to invest in prevention to make communities healthier."

2021–Today
Uneven Access in Developed Countries

As COVID-19 vaccines became available, many developed countries opened up access by age group. Adults older than 90 first, then the 80- to 90-year-olds and on down the line. Eventually every adult 18 years or older was eligible. Those who were anxiously waiting for the vaccine, myself included, registered for an appointment and went to get it. I am in a privileged group with access to the internet to make an appointment, access to transportation to get to the appointment and the means to take a few rest days from work if I feel any side effects. In short, it was easy for me to get vaccinated as soon as my age group was eligible.

But for millions of people in developed countries, it isn't easy to get vaccinated, even though they are eligible to get the vaccine. Some don't have a way to get to a vaccine clinic. Others are worried about taking time off work to go for vaccination. Still others are newcomers who aren't yet familiar with their new country's language and services. Many communities are realizing that they need to make it easier for people to get vaccinated. Community organizations and religious leaders can help people connect with vaccinators by holding clinics, spreading the word or providing services such as transportation or childcare.

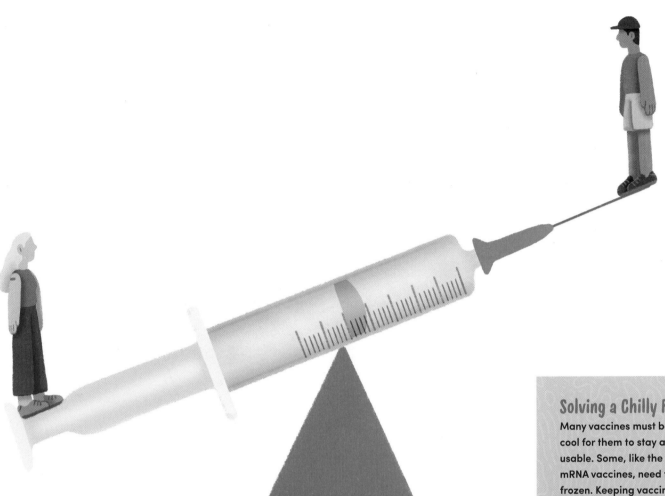

Future

Out of the Tropics

Developing vaccines takes a huge investment of money. Not surprisingly, vaccine makers want to sell their vaccines for enough money to make the investment worthwhile. But, as you read earlier, developing countries generally don't have much money to buy vaccines, and they often don't have the scientists and facilities to develop their own vaccines either. Many developing countries are in tropical regions of the world, with infectious diseases like Nipah virus and Zika virus. These diseases typically don't occur in cooler climates—which is where most of the vaccine makers are. To date, vaccine makers have ignored or invested little time and money into finding

vaccines for many of these diseases, which are often called "neglected tropical diseases."

With the climate crisis, some tropical diseases are moving to other regions of the world. For example, West Nile virus, first found in Africa, is now the most common disease carried by mosquitoes in the United States. Do you think vaccine makers will give neglected tropical diseases more attention if they become common in developed countries? Is this fair or ethical?

Solving a Chilly Problem

Many vaccines must be kept cool for them to stay active and usable. Some, like the COVID-19 mRNA vaccines, need to stay frozen. Keeping vaccines at the correct temperature can be difficult because it may take several weeks to ship a vaccine from the factory to a health clinic for injection into someone's arm. The task is especially difficult when the destination is a remote community with frequent power outages. This vaccine-delivery difficulty is called the cold-chain problem.

The ideal vaccine is thermostable, which means it stays active and usable even when the temperature changes. Researchers have created a few vaccines like this—the first was the smallpox vaccine. But making a thermostable vaccine isn't always easy depending on the type of vaccine. Researchers today are experimenting with methods like air-drying and freeze-drying, and work continues on finding ways to produce thermostable liquids.

1665
English villagers
quarantine
themselves
from the plague

1980s
The Global Polio
Eradication
Initiative

1938
March of Dimes
holds its first
fundrasier

2019
Teens for Vaccines
and VaxTeen start
raising awareness

TEN

RESPONSIBILITY

What We Can Do as Individuals

What are you responsible for at home? Perhaps washing the dinner dishes, taking out the garbage or making your bed. We all have responsibilities in life—some are responsibilities to ourselves, others to our family and friends, still others to our community. Vaccination fits into all three of these areas.

We owe it to ourselves to be protected against preventable diseases so we can live healthy lives and accomplish our goals. We owe it to our family and friends to be protected against preventable diseases because not everyone around us is able to be well protected by vaccines. Babies aren't old enough to be vaccinated against some diseases. Grandparents and other older people have weaker immune systems, so even when vaccinated, they're at greater risk than those of us who are younger.

Laughter between grandparent and grandchild is magical. But during the COVID-19 pandemic, many family members were isolated from one another and could only visit by phone or internet calls. When safe, effective COVID-19 vaccines became available, it allowed families to finally get together in person again.
KLAUS VEDFELT/GETTY IMAGES

We owe it to our community to be protected against preventable diseases because we live in communities with all kinds of people—some who can't be vaccinated because of a medical condition, others who are especially susceptible to disease or complications from getting sick. These people are protected only because the rest of us get vaccinated to keep cases of vaccine-preventable diseases low. That's the herd-immunity concept you read about earlier. If we don't get vaccinated, we make our community a more dangerous place.

We're all individuals, but none of us can survive alone. We're part of local, national and global communities, so we all have a moral responsibility to be vaccinated as our contribution to the health of these communities. How have communities responded in the past?

Will Polio Be Eradicated?

After smallpox was wiped out, world health leaders started looking at other diseases. The Global Polio Eradication Initiative began in the 1980s. At the time, 1,000 children were paralyzed by polio every day. Every day! With millions of volunteers vaccinating children worldwide, the initiative slowly declared region after region free of polio—the Americas in 1994, the Western Pacific in 2000, Europe in 2002. By 2006 only four countries remained on the list of places with wild-type poliovirus: Nigeria, India, Pakistan and Afghanistan.

Polio has been harder to eradicate than smallpox was, in part because of the way poliovirus works. Some people get polio and are asymptomatic, meaning they have no symptoms at all. This makes it difficult to isolate cases and stop others from being infected. Also, there are three strains of poliovirus, each needing a slightly different vaccine. Even so, the effort to get rid of polio was tantalizingly close—until COVID-19 appeared.

When COVID-19 disrupted the world, childhood vaccine programs were also interrupted. Pockets of unvaccinated or undervaccinated people have given polio a chance to infect more people. For the first time in many decades, public health departments in developed countries are urging people to make sure they have had the polio vaccine.

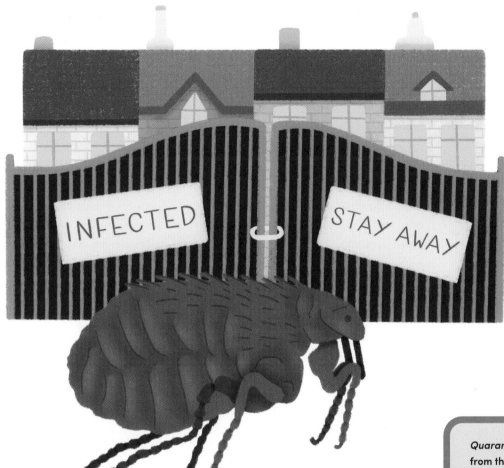

1665–1666
The Plague Village

In the English village of Eyam, the tailor ordered some materials from London in 1665. When the package arrived, it brought fleas infected with the plague. The tailor's assistant was the first villager to die of the Black Death. Over the next 14 months, 260 villagers died. This was between one-third and three-quarters of the villagers (estimates of the village population vary). In the 1660s nobody knew that bacteria caused the plague, but they understood how contagious it was. Guided by two religious leaders, the Eyam villagers agreed to try to keep the plague from spreading to nearby communities. They quarantined themselves by staying within the village boundary, and they put up signs warning travelers to stay away. Outsiders left food and supplies at the boundary in exchange for coins that the Eyam villagers placed in containers filled with vinegar. They knew that vinegar seemed to help kill the disease.

Centuries later epidemiologists— scientists who study patterns of disease— looked at the Eyam village records and mapped out who died and when during the 14-month plague outbreak. They found that three of every four people who died caught the plague from an infected person, so the sacrifice the villagers made in not leaving their village almost certainly prevented the disease from spreading to neighboring communities.

1900s–1950s
One Dime at a Time

As polio surfaced nearly every summer in the mid-1900s, parents worried about their children getting sick with this terrible disease. Desperate for a cure or a vaccine, parents across North America joined an annual campaign to raise money for polio research. These volunteers, most of them mothers, went around neighborhoods asking people to donate a dime—10 cents—to the National Foundation for Infantile Paralysis. (Polio used to be called infantile paralysis because it was originally thought to strike only infants and children, but we now know anyone can get the disease.)

The annual campaign was called the March of Dimes, and eventually the foundation changed its name to this catchy title. Teenagers also got in on the action, joining Teens Against Polio to collect donations. The research funded by all the dimes that poured in during these years eventually led to success with developing polio vaccines. All the time and effort that so many people gave to this campaign paid off as their own community and communities across the world became safer.

Margaret Lehand opens some of the 30,000 letters that arrived at the White House on January 28, 1938. Each letter contained a dime to support the work of the National Foundation for Infantile Paralysis. This foundation was started by then-president Franklin D. Roosevelt, who had been diagnosed with polio in 1921 and couldn't walk without help for the rest of his life.
WIKIMEDIA COMMONS/LIBRARY OF CONGRESS/PUBLIC DOMAIN

Life in an Echo Chamber

Have you ever been in a cave and shouted to hear your voice return in an echo? *Echo, echo, echo*, you hear as your voice bounces off the cave walls and grows fainter. Listening to an echo in a cave is fun, but how about on social media?

An echo chamber on social media happens when someone sees and reads only the exact same thoughts and opinions they already have. Imagine that you think penguins can fly. You look at your social media feeds, and everyone you follow thinks the same thing. People post pictures and stories of penguins flying. Chances are you'll keep this opinion about penguins. In this scenario, you're in an echo chamber, hearing and seeing what you already believe to be true. Except it's false.

Social media platforms are designed to feed us posts that are similar to posts we've already looked at or clicked on. The more we share posts from particular people or websites, the more we'll see posts from them in our feeds. These online echo chambers isolate us from other ideas and information. When this happens with false information about vaccines, some people get distorted views of vaccine safety and effectiveness, and they ignore or deny their responsibility to their community's health.

To avoid getting stuck in an echo chamber, try using lateral reading. That means searching for information on the same topic but written by different people and published in different places. This will give you a better idea of an author's credibility and the accuracy of their information. If several reliable sources all say the same thing, then the information is more likely to be true.

People who fall victim to an echo chamber filled with false information about vaccines are more likely to be vaccine hesitant.

Today

Vaccines as a Victim

In some ways vaccines are themselves a victim of how successfully they've squashed many infectious diseases. With the diseases out of sight, they're also out of mind. If we don't see sick people, we think the diseases aren't a threat anymore. But the only reason they're not a threat is because of vaccines. To keep diseases from returning, we need people to be vaccinated.

Please don't fall into the trap of thinking that because you're young and healthy, you don't need vaccines. You *do* need vaccines—to maintain your own health and that of your family, your friends and your community.

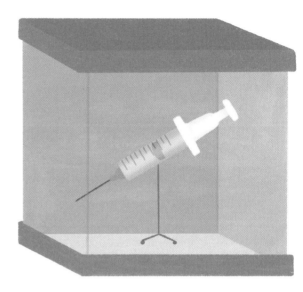

My daughter Madeleine can be pretty goofy!
ROWENA RAE

Today and into the Future: Playing Our Part

I hope this book gave you lots to think about and that you'll tell your friends and family what you now know about vaccination. Here are a few reminders and tips:

- Learn as much as you can about science, even if you don't want a career in science.

- Ask questions and think about the answers you find.

- Use critical thinking whenever you have a big decision to make.

- Read different types of media to find information, and use the five Ws to evaluate it.

- Look for medical information from sources that have true medical expertise.

- Be careful about what you post and "like" on social media.

- Become an ambassador for vaccines and vaccination.

Lastly, take a look at the career profiles in this book and consider whether you'd like to be in one of these professions—or another one related to infectious diseases and vaccines. There are many career paths in this area, and I couldn't include them all. No matter what career goals you have, what do you think you could do to help other people better understand infectious diseases and vaccines?

78

Teerka Baskaran

ANITA VASSERMAN

Cha Cha Yang

LOUIZA BOVAEVA

"Put yourself out there. Don't wait to be perfect or to have all the skills. Push out of your comfort zone."

"[Students] can become agents of change in their communities through peer-to-peer education."

Like many young people, Teerka Baskaran felt cooped up and restless at home during the COVID-19 pandemic lockdown. At one point she heard about an online meeting to talk about a new project, and she decided to attend. The meeting host was Cha Cha Yang, a recent university graduate in biology and the history of science. Yang had noticed that the pandemic brought two issues into the spotlight: vaccine hesitancy and mistrust of science.

"I realized that school students weren't learning about vaccines and immunization in their classrooms," says Yang. "I didn't either as a high school student in Toronto. It wasn't until I took a class at university that I really learned about vaccines." She decided to start an organization, along with her college roommate, called Frontline Immunity (formerly Students for Herd Immunity). The idea was to educate students in middle and high school about the science of vaccines so they would have accurate information. Frontline Immunity also helps students gain the confidence and skills to become vaccine ambassadors—people who speak with their peers, families and others in their community about what they've learned.

The online meeting sparked Baskaran's interest. "Cha Cha was inviting students to get involved," she says. "It was the first time someone said I could actually do something." Baskaran participated in the pilot program—a workshop Yang created with input from scientists, doctors and other partners—and became a vaccine ambassador while she was in ninth grade. "It was all about having students talk to students," says Baskaran. "After the program, I shared information with a friend I wanted to hang out with. It helped my friend take more ownership about wanting to get the [COVID-19] vaccine."

So far more than 500 students at about 200 schools in Canada and the United States have taken Frontline Immunity's workshop. The organization estimates that about 200,000 students and 900,000 people overall have heard from one of the ambassadors about the importance of vaccination and the need to tackle vaccine misinformation.

Baskaran now helps out with some of Frontline Immunity's projects by participating as a member of the youth advisory board. She's a high school student working hard with an eye to a career in public health, but even though she is busy, it's also important to Baskaran to keep giving some of her time to the organization. "So many people helped my family and me when we immigrated to Canada," she says. "This is a way of giving back to make community supports even stronger."

GLOSSARY

anaphylaxis—a serious allergic reaction to something a person touches or that enters the body in food or by some other means

antibodies—proteins that the body makes in the bloodstream to fight pathogens

antitoxin—a treatment that cancels the negative effect of a poisonous or toxic substance

autoimmune disorders—conditions in which the immune system mistakes healthy body cells for unfriendly cells and attacks them. Examples are multiple sclerosis, rheumatoid arthritis and type 1 diabetes.

bacteria (singular: *bacterium*)—small, single-celled organisms that live in soil, water, plants and animals, including humans. Some but not all bacteria are pathogens.

binary fission—a simple method used by some organisms to multiply, or reproduce, where the parent organism divides into two identical new organisms

cancers—illnesses that occur when certain cells in the body grow out of control and invade other parts of the body. Without treatment, cancers will eventually kill the affected animal or person.

cells—the smallest things that can live on their own. All plants and animals are made up of cells.

clinical trials—scientific research studies that test a new medicine or vaccine for safety and effectiveness in people

communities—in biology, groups of different species that live in the same place at the same time and interact with one another

contagious—easily spread from one individual to another

contaminate—to make something unclean or unfit for use by adding a dirty or dangerous thing to it

developed countries—countries in which most people have a good standard of living because there is industrial activity and a strong economy

developing countries—countries in which most people live on small amounts of money because there isn't much industrial activity to boost the economy

disinformation—false information that is spread deliberately to influence other people

DNA—a complex structure in cells that is shaped like a twisted ladder and carries the inherited instructions for how an organism looks and functions. Spelled out as *deoxyribonucleic acid.*

epidemic—a disease that affects many people at the same time in a community or region

eradicate—to get rid of or destroy something completely

fungi (singular: *fungus*)—organisms that live on decaying material or on plants and animals. Examples are molds, mushrooms and yeasts. Some but not all fungi are pathogens.

herd immunity—a reduction in the ability of a disease to spread through a community because most individuals are immune to the disease, either from previous exposure or from vaccination. Also called *community immunity.*

HIV/AIDS—the term used to describe acquired immunodeficiency syndrome (AIDS), a condition caused by the human immunodeficiency virus (HIV) attacking the body's immune system

hypothesis—an explanation or idea that can be tested with an experiment to find out if it might be correct

immune—protected from getting a particular infection or disease

immune system—the parts of the body that work together to protect the body from infection and disease

immunity—the body's ability to protect itself from infection and disease

infections—conditions caused by pathogens that have entered the body

infectious diseases—diseases caused when pathogens enter the body and then grow and multiply there

informed consent—agreement to participate in something, such as a clinical trial, surgery or other medical procedure, after receiving and understanding information about the risks and benefits

inherited—passed from parent to child. In biology, DNA is passed from each parent to their child, so the child has characteristics that are similar to their those of their parents.

killed vaccines—vaccines made with a pathogen that has been killed by heat or chemicals. Also called *inactivated vaccines*.

laws—long-term rules that a government puts in place telling people what they must or must not do. See *mandates*.

live, weakened vaccines—vaccines made with a pathogen that has been weakened but not killed. Also called *live, attenuated vaccines*.

mandates—short-term rules a government puts in place requiring people to do a particular task because of a particular situation. See *laws*.

microbes—very small organisms that can be seen only with a microscope. Also called *microorganisms*.

microscope—an instrument that uses lenses to make small objects look larger so it's easier to examine them

misinformation—incorrect or misleading information

mutate—to develop new characteristics because of a change in an organism's inherited instructions, called *DNA* (or *RNA* in the case of some viruses)

nucleus—the central part of a cell that contains the DNA in plants and animals

pandemic—a disease that spreads across a wide geographic area

pasteurization—the process of heating a liquid, often milk, to a certain temperature and then cooling it to kill bacteria

pathogens—things that cause infection and disease. Also called *germs*.

populations—in biology, groups of a single species that live in the same place at the same time

proteins—substances in living things that are necessary for life and have many different jobs, including carrying messages, giving structure to cells and moving things around

protozoa (singular: *protozoan*)—small, single-celled animals. Some but not all protozoa are pathogens.

quarantine—a period of time that a person or animal who definitely has or possibly has a disease must stay away from others to prevent the disease from spreading

ribosome—a small structure in cells where proteins are made

RNA—a structure similar to DNA but with only one strand. There are several types of RNA, including messenger RNA (mRNA). In viruses, RNA sometimes carries the inherited instructions instead of DNA. Spelled out as *ribonucleic acid*.

species—a set of organisms that has similar characteristics and can breed with each other

vaccination—the process of giving a person or an animal a vaccine to protect them from getting a particular disease

vaccine candidate—a vaccine that has not gone through the full set of testing and clinical trials to determine its safety and effectiveness

vaccines—substances put into a person or animal that prompt their body to form antibodies to protect them from getting a particular disease

variant—something that looks or functions slightly differently from another form of the same thing

variolation—a technique to deliberately infect a person with a small amount of smallpox virus to protect them from getting smallpox in the future

ventilator—a machine that pushes air into a person's lungs when they can no longer breathe on their own

viruses—extremely small infectious agents that consist of a piece of DNA or RNA wrapped in a coat of protein. They can multiply only in the cells of a host plant or animal, so viruses are considered to be nonliving. However, they get included with other microbes when talking about infectious diseases. Some but not all viruses are pathogens.

zoonoses—diseases caused by pathogens that spread from animals to humans

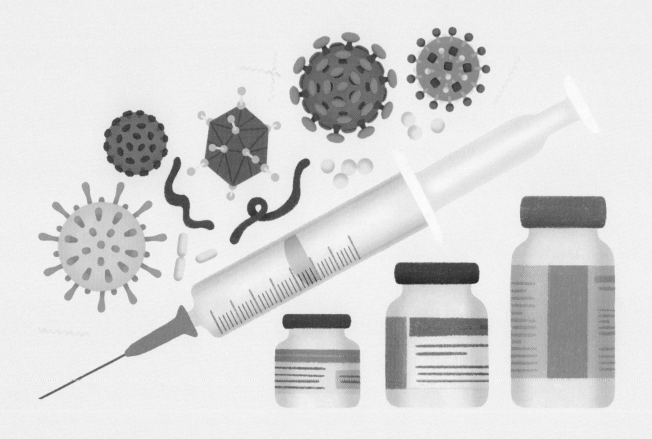

RESOURCES

Print

Brown, Don. *A Shot in the Arm!* Amulet Books, 2021.

Caulfield, Timothy. *The Vaccination Picture.* Viking, 2017.

Haelle, Tara. *Vaccination Investigation: The History and Science of Vaccines.* Twenty-First Century Books, 2018.

King-Cargile, Gillian. *Vaccines Change the World.* Albert Whitman and Company, 2022.

Marrin, Albert. *Very, Very, Very Dreadful: The Influenza Pandemic of 1918.* Knopf Books for Young Readers, 2018.

Peters, Marilee. *Patient Zero: Solving the Mysteries of Deadly Epidemics,* updated edition. Annick Press, 2021.

Wright, Jennifer. *Get Well Soon: History's Worst Plagues and the Heroes Who Fought Them.* Henry Holt and Company, 2017.

Online

Frontline Immunity: frontlineimmunity.com

High School Bioethics Project, NYU: med.nyu.edu/departments-institutes/population-health/divisions-sections-centers/medical-ethics/education/high-school-bioethics-project

History of Vaccines, from the College of Physicians of Philadelphia: historyofvaccines.org

Indigenous Pharmacy Professionals of Canada: pharmacists.ca/pharmacy-in-canada/ippc

Kids Boost Immunity (a resource that pairs student learning with a global reward: vaccines for children in need through UNICEF): kidsboostimmunity.com

News Literacy Project: newslit.org

Teen Fact-Checking Network: poynter.org/mediawise/programs/tfcn

Teens for Vaccines: teensforvaccines.org

Vaccine Education Center, Children's Hospital of Philadelphia: chop.edu/centers-programs/vaccine-education-center

Vaccine Information You Need, from Immunize.org in partnership with the Centers for Disease Control and Prevention: vaccineinformation.org

Vaccine Safety Net, from the WHO (a global network of websites with reliable information on vaccine safety): vaccinesafetynet.org

Vaccines and Immunizations, from the Centers for Disease Control and Prevention: cdc.gov/vaccines

VaxTeen: vaxteen.org

Voices for Vaccines: voicesforvaccines.org

APP

Vaccines on the Go: What You Should Know, by the Vaccine Education Center, Children's Hospital of Philadelphia

ACKNOWLEDGMENTS

I owe special thanks to my mother, Ann Skidmore, who raised me to have a healthy respect for infectious diseases. Even today, decades retired from her career as an infectious diseases physician, she still gives me information about the latest vaccines and recommendations. She also read and commented on an early draft of this book. Thank you, Maman!

Two other professionals reviewed the text as well and gave me excellent suggestions and advice that improved the book. My thanks to Gretchen LaSalle, a family physician in Spokane, WA, and author of *Let's Talk Vaccines* (Wolters Kluwer, 2020), and to Charlotte Moser, co-director of the Vaccine Education Center at the Children's Hospital of Philadelphia and co-author with Paul Offit of *Vaccines and Your Child* (Columbia University Press, 2011). I'm extremely grateful to them for their time and helpful comments. Any mistakes, however, are mine.

I also thank the twelve people who spoke with me about their careers and who agreed to be included in the book. They are Akarin Asavajaru, vaccine research technician, Saskatchewan; Alexandre White, medical historian, Maryland; Brendan Parent, medical ethicist, New York; Cha Cha Yang, graduate student and co-founder of Frontline Immunity, Ontario; Inci Yildirim, pediatric infectious disease specialist and vaccinologist, Connecticut; Jaris Swidrovich, clinical and research pharmacist, Ontario; Mallory Bergum, community health nurse, Yukon; Prativa Baral, international health epidemiologist, Quebec; Shehzad Iqbal, medical director, Ontario; Tatiana Arias, clinical trials manager, Quebec; Teerka Baskaran, high school student and volunteer with Frontline Immunity, Ontario; and Young Anna Argyris, information systems researcher, Michigan. Several others also helped me connect with these people. My thanks to Amaris Poznikoff, Arinjay Banerjee, James Burns, Jessica Rivera, Maria Nyland, Sacha Kennedy and Trenna Brusky. Daniel Peach at the University of Georgia helped me with mosquito identification.

While researching this book, I read or listened to many interesting books written for adults, and I consulted many organizations' websites. A list of these is available on the page for this book at orcabook.com.

The team at Orca Book Publishers is fantastic to work with. Thank you to my editor, Kirstie Hudson, for her guidance and patience, and to the many others in the Orca Pod who work so hard to produce beautiful and informative books, among them editorial assistant Georgia Bradburne, production editor Mark Grill, marketing coordinators Olivia Gutjahr and Mya Colwell, copyeditor Vivian Sinclair and proofreader Audrey McClellan. I'm also so grateful to have worked with illustrator Paige Stampatori and designer Dahlia Yuen. The fabulous look of this book is due to their outstanding work.

Last, but far from least, I thank my family for their boundless encouragement and support while I was working on this book. Thank you, all!

INDEX

*Page numbers in **bold** indicate an image caption.*

Rowena Rae worked as a biologist in Canada and New Zealand before becoming a freelance writer, editor, trainer and children's author. She is the author of *Salmon: Swimming for Survival* in the Orca Wild series and *Upstream, Downstream: Exploring Watershed Connections* and *Chemical World: Science in Our Daily Lives* in the Orca Footprints series. She also wrote *Rachel Carson and Ecology for Kids*. Rowena writes both fiction and nonfiction from her home in Victoria, British Columbia.

Paige Stampatori is an illustrator based in Kitchener, Ontario. She graduated from Sheridan College's Illustration program in 2020. Typically working in editorial illustration, Paige loves to create graphic, colorful images that are conceptually strong. Her favorite part of the creative process is the ideation stage. She finds it exciting to think of interesting ways to convey a message through a single image.

From the PAST to the PRESENT AND INTO the FUTURE!

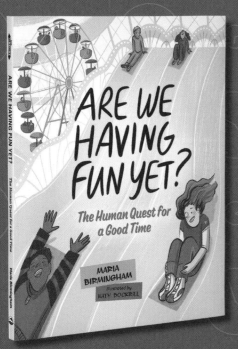

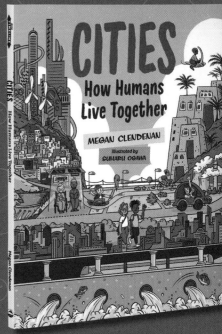

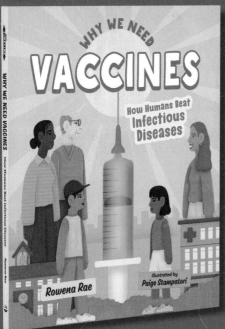

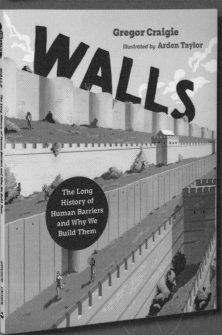

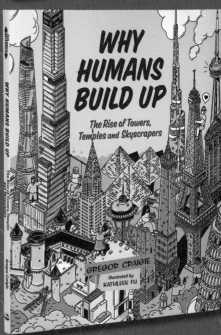

The **Orca TIMELINE** series explores how big ideas have shaped humanity. Discover what our collective history can tell us about the planet today and tomorrow.